11/02

PEOPLE AT ODDS

THE IRA AND ENGLAND

PEOPLE AT ODDS

PEOPLE AT ODDS

THE IRA AND ENGLAND

Heather Lehr Wagner

Chelsea House Publishers
Philadelphia

CHELSEA HOUSE PUBLISHERS

EDITOR IN CHIEF Sally Cheney
DIRECTOR OF PRODUCTION Kim Shinners
CREATIVE MANAGER Takeshi Takahashi
MANUFACTURING MANAGER Diann Grasse

Staff for THE IRA AND ENGLAND

ASSISTANT EDITOR Susan Naab
PICTURE RESEARCHER Sarah Bloom
PRODUCTION ASSISTANT Jaimie Winkler
SERIES AND COVER DESIGNER Keith Trego
LAYOUT 21st Century Publishing and Communications, Inc.

http://www.chelseahouse.com

First Printing

1 3 5 7 9 8 6 4 2

Library of Congress Cataloging-in-Publication Data

Wagner, Heather Lehr.
   The IRA and England / by Heather Wagner.
      p. cm. — (People at odds)
Summary: Discusses the background and development of the conflict
between the Irish Republican Army fighting for the Catholics in Ireland
and the British government forces supporting the Irish Protestants.
Includes bibliographical references and index.
   ISBN 0-7910-6706-8
 1. Irish Republican Army—History—Juvenile literature. 2. Ireland—
History—20th century—Juvenile literature. 3. Political violence—Ireland
—History—20th century—Juvenile literature. 4. Political violence—
Northern Ireland—History—Juvenile literature. 5. Ireland—History,
Military—20th century—Juvenile literature. 6. Northern Ireland—History,
Military—Juvenile literature. 7. Ireland—Relations—England—Juvenile
literature. 8. England—Relations—Ireland—Juvenile literature.
[1. Ireland—History—20th century. 2. Irish Republican Army—History.
3. Ireland—Relations—England. 4. England—Relations—Ireland.]
I. Title. II. Series.
DA959 .W34 2002
941.6082—dc21

                                                          2001007938

CONTENTS

The Lines are Drawn

I t was at eleven o'clock on the morning of October 11, 1921, that Michael Collins began the process that would tear Ireland apart. The 30-year-old Irishman and four of his countrymen had come to London to negotiate a peace treaty to end the violence that had ravaged an Ireland desperate for independence from Britain.

Collins was a soldier, not a diplomat, but into his hands had been trusted one of the most important roles in recent Irish history—meeting with the British to carve out the path to peace. The people wanted an end to the fierce fighting that had transformed their countryside into a battlefield. As the team from Ireland headed for the meeting, they found the London streets lined with men, women and children praying. Immigrants from Ireland who had found a home in England turned out in

The map of Europe reflects many changes that have occurred in the last half-century, but Northern Ireland remains a part of the United Kingdom.

A granite crucifix marks the spot where Michael Collins was ambushed and killed by fellow Republicans in his home county of Cork on August 22, 1922.

force to cheer on their countrymen. Flags waved, and nuns and priests stood on the streets calling out blessings. The hopes of their people rested on the shoulders of this inexperienced group of soldiers and revolutionaries.

The discomfort of Collins was magnified when he entered the impressive setting and faced the British negotiating team. The location of the meeting—Downing Street—was the first step in the intimidation process. The British had challenged and mastered many other opponents in that impressive setting, and the walls were lined with portraits of the men who had carved out the mighty British Empire.

The team sent to represent the British side was as impressive as the setting. Britain was one of the world's foremost powers, and the men seated at the table had helped make it so. There was the British Prime Minister, David Lloyd George, the Lord Chancellor Birkenhead, the Chancellor of the Exchequer (chief finance minister) Sir Austen Chamberlain, and the Colonial Secretary Winston Churchill. As if this experienced team of the great political minds of Britain was not enough, its side also included the Chief Secretary for Ireland, the War Secretary and the Attorney General.

This team of elite politicians, in this impressive setting, gazed across the table at Michael Collins, a fugitive from justice, a man for whose capture a reward of 10,000 British pounds sterling had been offered. The British had come to preserve the peace in a strategically important corner of their empire, to negotiate through diplomacy what they had not been able to achieve through force. Michael Collins had come to sort out the process by which Ireland could become a republic, capable of governing itself.

Over the next several weeks, in seven formal meetings, 24 sub-conferences, nine informal meetings and frequent correspondence, a treaty was gradually outlined. The treaty granted Ireland dominion status, bringing it in line with other British outposts such as Canada and New Zealand, and giving it the right to form its own Parliament. This new dominion would be known as the Irish Free State. But there were two sticking points that brought dissension to the negotiating table. The treaty required all members of the newly

David Lloyd George (1863-1945) was the British Prime Minister who negotiated the treaty that split Ireland into two areas: the Irish Free State and Northern Ireland.

formed Irish Parliament to swear an oath of allegiance to the British king. And the treaty split Ireland into two areas: the Irish Free State and Northern Ireland. The six counties of Northern Ireland would be given one month to decide whether or not they wished to join the Irish Free State. If, within that time, they determined to remain tied to Britain, the laws of the Irish Free State and the right of self-rule would not extend past the borders of Northern Ireland. The boundary lines would be determined by three representatives: one from the Irish Free State, one from the government of Northern Ireland, and one appointed by the British government.

Strangely enough, it was the idea of swearing an oath to the British king that was the more troublesome of these two points to the group from Ireland. The idea of splitting off a portion of their country and keeping it tied to Britain bothered them less, perhaps because they believed that in one month's time they could persuade their fellow countrymen to accept the terms of the treaty and join the forces demanding independence. They also felt no need to force independence on any portion of their land—those who wished to be free could choose to do so.

And so, after consultation with the other members of the Irish Republican Brotherhood (the group that had led the move for a free state) still back in Dublin, Collins and the others reluctantly agreed to the terms of the treaty. They did so still worrying about the impact of the oath, but believing that the partition of their country might never take place. Collins also knew that the war he had helped to command needed to stop. His weapons supply was low, the leaders of the Irish side were all marked men, there had been many deaths on both sides, and the people's enthusiasm for the fight was ebbing.

The team returned to Ireland to be viewed not as heroes but as traitors. As they had predicted, the idea of swearing an oath to the British king was viewed with horror. The same group of politicians who had insisted they attend and negotiate now distanced themselves quickly. Collins had been set up. There had been no way to end the war except through compromise, but Collins was one of the few who had been willing to put his name to the compromise and then work forward.

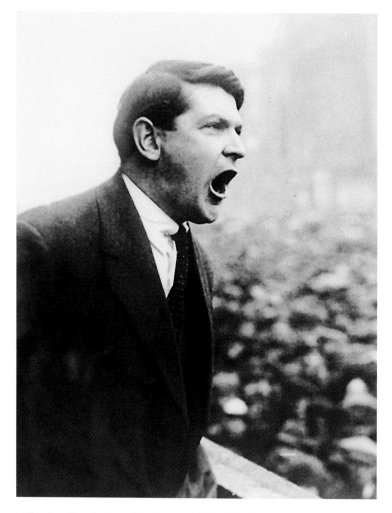

Following the signing of the treaty, Michael Collins struggled to win his countrymen's acceptance of the plan to achieve Ireland's independence. Here, he speaks before a crowd gathered for a treaty meeting in Dublin on March 18, 1922.

After bitter fighting amongst the leaders of the Irish Republican Brotherhood, the Treaty finally passed on January 7, 1922. It was the hope of all those involved that four years of violence had come to an end. They were to be tragically mistaken.

For as that year of 1922 unfolded, Ireland would erupt in civil war. What began with the signing of a treaty dividing Ireland into two would result in violence and bloodshed that continue to this day. The group of politicians and soldiers who had achieved a hard-fought independence from Britain would split into two, just as their country did, and fight each other with the same intensity with which they had fought their British foes.

And Michael Collins, the Commander in Chief of the Irish Republican Army, would be killed, not by the British soldiers he plotted against for so long, but by a fellow Irishman, in an ambush set in a remote corner of Northern Ireland.

THE SEEDS OF REVOLUTION

What brought Michael Collins and his fellow republicans to their tragic end? Their dreams of a united and independent Ireland were first hatched in prison. As the murmurs and whispers calling for a free, republican Ireland grew louder, the British retaliated with violence and harsh measures. Imprisonment without trial was a common practice, and the British policing Ireland were adept at seizing those suspected of fanning the flames of revolution, throwing them into jail and often executing them.

For a young Michael Collins, coming of age in Ireland at the beginning of the 20th century meant being surrounded by tales of horror and loss at the hands of the harsh British occupiers. Land was seized, friends and relatives were suddenly tossed into prison, and the one language that both sides seemed to communicate best in was violence. By 1916, the British indifference to the conditions of Irishmen had resulted in a Dublin full of slums, with high unemployment and high infant mortality. Britain's entry into World War I, under the guise of fighting for the rights of small nations, had sparked hope that the "small nation" of Ireland would benefit at the end of the war through recognition of its own rights. But by Easter of 1916, it had become clear that loyalty to the Empire would result only in a continuation of the conditions that kept the Irish population subservient to a distant king. The prospect of a draft in which young Irish men would be called to fight to defend the rights of an empire that refused to admit their own rights sparked great outrage.

The fighting was launched on Easter, as various important buildings and monuments in Dublin were seized by a group of rebels, the 26-year-old Michael Collins among them. The fighting between British troops and Irish rebels was intense, with machine-gun and rifle fire echoing through the streets and buildings being burned. The British brought in gunboats, and as flames and bullets devastated the city, the outmanned rebels were eventually forced to surrender.

The fate of the revolution lay in the hands of the British at this point. Had they treated their prisoners humanely, had they made some attempt to respond to the conditions that sparked the fighting, all might have been saved. But instead, the British responded with brutality and humiliation—tactics that would not be forgotten by the Irish witnesses. Prisoners were stripped naked, beaten, many placed quickly before the firing squad without a trial. Those who were not immediately executed were sent to labor prisons in England or Ireland.

These prisons would prove the fertile ground upon which the seeds of revolution first sprouted. Men with little in common before were thrust together in horrible conditions, treated brutally and subjected to torture. Some men were

Following the 1916 Easter Rising in Dublin, British forces imprisoned Irish rebel fighters in internment camps like this one and subjected them to inhumane treatment, torture and even execution.

broken, but others formed a sense of comraderie that would inspire them to fight back against the British and stand together to win their independence.

As prisoners were released or escaped, they carried back tales of the brutal conditions and the inhumane treatment they had suffered. Just at this sensitive time, the British, in an attempt to address the rebellion, determined to grant Ireland some limited powers. The proposal set forward was that Ireland would be allowed to form a parliament, but it could not direct the activities of its army or navy. Nor would the British allow Ireland to direct its own postal service, customs or taxation. Slightly less than half (40 percent) of the seats of the newly formed parliament must be given to unionists—those who supported a continued union with Britain. At the same time, a military service bill would be passed instituting a draft.

The draft would prove Britain's tragic mistake. Resistance immediately mounted, as Irishmen recently released from British prisons refused to be drafted to fight to protect the British Empire. The signing of the armistice with Germany brought an end to World War I, but the threat of the draft remained. Sensing that hostilities were growing, Britain decided to crack down further, banning the Irish from carrying weapons, engaging in military drills, and even holding Irish language classes, soccer games or dancing competitions.

As Britain entered the Paris Peace Conference to negotiate the terms of the end of World War I, the eyes of its leaders turned away from Ireland. As their focus shifted in those months of 1919, the Irish revolutionaries moved forward. They would not settle for small gestures. They wanted nothing short of independence.

THE BIRTH OF THE IRA

On April 10, 1919, the newly formed Irish Parliament met to lay out their plans for independence. The meeting contained a Declaration of Independence, a program for democracy, and a message to the "Free Nations of the World." Perhaps more significantly, it was at this meeting that the group of volunteers who had banded together to fight the British was formalized into the Irish Republican Army, a name that would eventually be shortened to IRA. Many of those who had suffered in British prisons had vowed never to return, and declared that they would fight to resist any future arrest.

The evidence of injustice could be summarized in stark numbers. Between 1917 and 1918, the number of arrests had increased from 347 to 1107, the number of English raids had grown from 11 to 260, and the number of deportations (where Irish prisoners were sent to English jails) had risen from 24 to 91. Twelve newspapers had been forced to halt printing, numerous meetings had been suppressed, and the number of times Irishmen had faced British soldiers at bayonet point, or had been clubbed by sticks, had quadrupled.

But the troubles would grow much worse. In Ireland, the year 1920 is remembered as a year of terror. The few thousand who formed the IRA began to paralyze Ireland with raids, with rallies, with daring plans to spring Irishmen from prison and with guerilla attacks against British soldiers and policemen. They had the support of ordinary people, who would assist them in their campaign to force the independence issue. The British responded by sending in a team of fighters intended to end the rebellion once and for all. Advertisements placed in British newspapers for men willing to undertake a "rough and dangerous task" had resulted in a makeshift army who arrived in Ireland and immediately began a shoot-to-kill policy. This group, known as the Black and Tans for the black and brown khaki uniforms they wore, unleashed a new campaign of terror in the streets of Ireland. A string of trucks would pull into a city, the Black and Tans would get out and immediately begin shooting. Their apparent goal—to make Ireland a nightmare for the rebels and IRA forces—succeeded instead in making Ireland a nightmare for the entire population.

And with that, the war was on. The fighting intensified throughout 1920 and reached its height in 1921. Using spies and propaganda, both sides created a climate of fury and hate in their people. The IRA fought most successfully with ambushes, attacking military barracks late at night with small teams of 15 to 20 men. They succeeded in pushing back the British forces not because of their numbers or weapons, but instead because of the support they received from the local people, who fed them and, more importantly, hid them.

Uncertain where IRA sympathizers might be found, the British reacted by attacking anyone suspected of supporting the rebels. Priests were no safer than anyone else; aware of the strong pro-Catholic nature of the IRA, priests were considered a source of IRA support and were frequently shot. Nuns responded by hiding wounded members of the IRA in maternity hospitals where they could safely receive medical care. Members of the IRA who were captured were subjected to horrific torture before being executed. Martial law was eventually declared, and thousands more British troops were ordered into Ireland to police the streets.

One of the leaders of the IRA, Terence MacSwiney, summarized the climate of the times: "It is not those who can inflict the most, but those than can suffer the most who will conquer." MacSwiney's words were prophetic. Following his arrest in 1921, he would go on a hunger strike to protest his court martial. It would end in his death 74 days later.

A TRUCE IS DECLARED

By the middle of 1921, both sides were beginning to look for a peaceful solution to the fighting. The British had suffered in the eyes of the world as their attempts to put

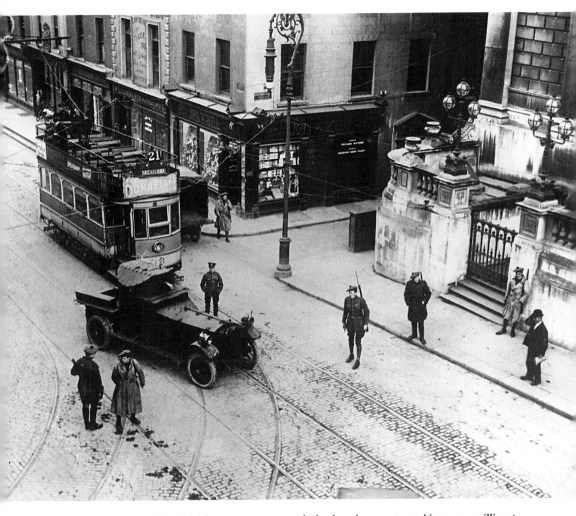

In 1920, British newspapers carried advertisements seeking men willing to undertake a "rough and dangerous task." This makeshift army, known as the Black and Tans for the black and brown khaki uniforms they wore, unleashed a new campaign of terror in the streets of Ireland.

down the Irish rebellion had been met with international criticism. The IRA, in turn, was suffering from a loss of lives and weapons. Both sides were eager to negotiate.

A truce was finally agreed upon, to go into effect at noon on July 11, 1921. The British agreed to halt the arrival of additional troops, police and weapons, as well as to stop obvious troop movements or displays of force. They also agreed to stop their efforts to hunt down IRA men or weapons. In turn, the Irish agreed to halt their attacks on British forces and civilians, to end their attacks on British property, and to avoid any other "displays of force." The agreement did not require the IRA to turn over their weapons, or to disband.

The truce was the first step in the process that would bring Michael Collins to the negotiating table in London a brief three months later.

AN IMPOSSIBLE PEACE

The forces that shaped Ireland's destiny in the early part of the 20th century made it practically impossible for peace to succeed. Centuries of oppression were not easily forgotten; the loss of friends and family members was not quickly forgiven.

Protestants who had come to settle the northern Irish shores under the protection of King James I had strong ties to Britain. They feared being swallowed up and becoming a religious minority in Ireland. The six counties that were to form Northern Ireland became a new battleground in the weeks after the Irish parliament finally approved the treaty that Collins had negotiated.

Loyalists in Northern Ireland quickly organized, with British backing, a strong political force to ensure that their region would remain separate and apart from the Irish free state. By the end of 1921, a split was at work in the south as well, with republicans who felt Ireland must stand free and united drawing apart from those who (like Collins) felt that compromise was the only way forward. The country erupted into civil war.

The IRA joined the fighting in Northern Ireland, combating the efforts of the British and Unionists to create six Protestant counties that would spell doom for any Catholics living within the borders. Through violence and illegal rigging of voting districts and boundaries, the Protestants took steps to ensure that a Protestant majority existed in each and every region, a majority that would vote to stay with Britain, rather than join the Irish free state. Catholics were ousted from their homes, which were then burned.

By May 1922, the IRA was retaliating with force. Now it was Protestant property that was burned, principally in Belfast. The IRA's policy was an immediate response to any Unionist attacks, with a reprisal rate of six to one. If one Catholic was shot, six Unionists would be executed in return. If a Catholic home was burned, six Protestant homes would be immediately torched.

The result was a Northern region devastated by violence, by death, by unemployment and homelessness. As Commander in Chief of the IRA, Collins sensed that the years of fighting were wearing on the people, and southern support for IRA activities was dwindling. While the people had stood solidly behind the IRA's campaign against British troops, they were less willing to support years of violence against other Irishmen. One by one, many leading figures who had led the rebellion were dead or imprisoned. Collins would be next.

In August of 1922, Michael Collins set out for Cork, a territory where IRA support was at its weakest. He wanted to put in an appearance there to bolster the morale of the IRA soldiers, and also hoped that such an appearance would win additional financial and public support for the campaign for independence. In addition, he wanted to return to Cork, for it was where he had been born, and he wanted once more to touch base with his fellow Corkians, revisit some familiar pubs and talk to some old friends and relatives.

In 1922, Ireland erupted into civil war. Here, soldiers from the Irish Free State are shown firing an 18-pound artillery cannon against Republican forces.

His nostalgic homeward journey would prove a tragic mistake. With only a small military escort to protect him, Collins was ambushed on a remote stretch of country road on the night of August 22, 1922. He was shot not by British forces, nor by Unionist militants, but instead by a group of Republicans who disagreed with the treaty Collins had helped negotiate, who resented the involvement of southern leaders in northern affairs, but whose goals, tragically, were not terribly dissimilar to those of Collins.

The death of Collins did not bring an end to the civil war. It did not bring victory to either side. Instead, the gap between southern and northern Ireland widened. And the violence and strife between the IRA and England would result in many more deaths.

The War Years

The civil war that split Ireland in two at the beginning of the 20th century did not arise spontaneously but had its history in centuries of conflict and oppression. Like many other British colonies and territories, Ireland suffered from the split between those who upheld the right of a distant king to rule over their land, and the preference of a people to determine their own destiny. As the 20th century took shape, Britain found itself confronted on several continents by cries for independence and an inability to keep so many different outposts in check while, simultaneously, fighting two world wars. The solution in many cases, as in Ireland, was to create borders, to separate lands that had once been united. The borders drawn that separated areas of the Middle East, that divided India and Pakistan, and that split Ireland in two, would continue to be flashpoints of violence well after the 20th century had ended.

But the partition of Ireland, and the subsequent violence

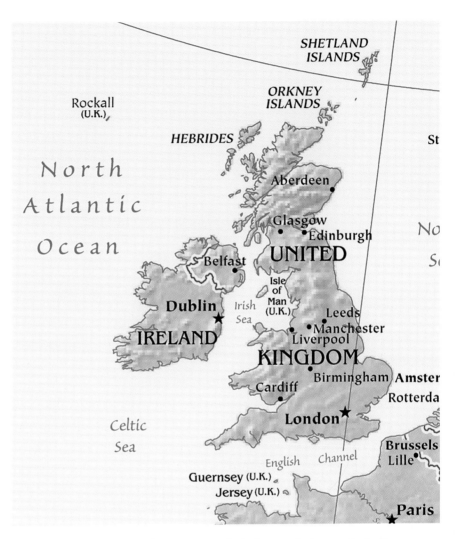

Northern Ireland's proximity to Great Britain has made it a strategically important part of the United Kingdom.

in Northern Ireland, split the island into communities, as well as counties, and it is in these communities that the violence continues to this day. The communities, for the most part, have been defined along religious lines, and religious beliefs have shaped political values, with

Protestants supporting a continuing link with Britain and Catholics supporting a completely independent Ireland. Why?

The history of conflict that separated Catholics and Protestants dates back to the 1600s, to the time of King James I, who set aside six counties in northeastern Ireland to be settled by Protestants, for the most part Presbyterians from Scotland. The land there was not uninhabited territory, and so the result of King James' grant to new settlers was that many farmers and landowners were forced from their homes to make way for the new settlers. This would prove the beginning of centuries of wars— wars fought over land, but dividing the population by religion.

On July 12, 1690, the Battle of the Boyne was won— a date that is still a source of celebration in Northern Ireland for the Protestant community. The battle was won by the army of William of Orange, who established a Protestant government in Ireland. For the next hundred years, the Catholics in Ireland were subjected to the tyranny of a Protestant ruling class, until in 1791 a young student named Wolfe Tone wrote a pamphlet called *An Argument on Behalf of the Catholics in Ireland*. Tone was a Protestant and he quickly formed a group of like-minded young men who vowed to unite Irishmen of all faiths in a common effort to win their independence from England. Had this group, the United Irishmen, been successful in their efforts, Ireland's history would have been quite different.

But the movement did not succeed. It served instead to further divide communities, and to increase the British presence in Ireland. Wealthy Protestants, concerned at the potential disruption to their profitable links to

Every July 12, Protestants in Northern Ireland celebrate the victory of the Battle of the Boyne, which led to William of Orange's establishing a Protestant government in Ireland in 1690. Members of the Orange Order, like this man with his child, march through the streets in a parade that frequently leads to violent confrontations between Protestant and Catholic communities.

England and to the challenge to a system from which they had benefited, quickly rallied together to form their own group. This group was known as the Orange Order, a nod to the history that had first dictated a Protestant rule for Ireland. Their goal was to maintain the peace and the existing laws—laws that were quite favorable to Protestants.

The Orange Order exists in the North to this day, where it remains a powerful political force. Membership in the Order guarantees certain jobs and preferred housing. And each year the Orange Order stages a march through the streets on July 12—a march that can become a rallying cry for both sides, a parade that often erupts in violence as each side views the other through the banners of a bloody history.

Wolfe Tone did not survive the revolution he started, nor would the revolution ultimately be successful. But the views first published in his pamphlet remain alive in many in northern Ireland, and the spirit of his movement would go on to thrive in the IRA.

THE ECONOMICS OF PARTITION

With the division of Ireland into an independent Republic of Ireland in the south and the six counties in the north linked to Britain, the two sides set off on very different paths of development. The global economic depression was strongly felt in Northern Ireland, where industries like shipbuilding suffered greatly and unemployment began to swallow more and more of the population. Britain soon extended many of the same programs to Northern Ireland that were being offered to citizens in England—for example, health insurance and unemployment benefits.

While such programs helped address some of the economic hardships the region was experiencing on a short-term basis, it also began a dangerous, dependent relationship, increasing the resentment both of the citizens of Northern Ireland—who believed (often correctly) that the payments and benefits they were receiving were inferior to those granted to people living in Britain—and of the residents of Britain, who were experiencing their own economic struggles in the aftermath of World War I and did not wish to see their taxes supporting the same Irishmen who had fought so violently against British troops.

While the conflict in Northern Ireland has its roots in many factors, economics played an important role in shaping the early days after Ireland's partition. The two sides have often been reduced to religious terms—"Protestants" and "Catholics"—or to political terms—"loyalists" and "republicans" or "unionists" and "nationalists"—but the reality is more complicated. Labels can be misleading, and when groups of people are divided into religious groups like Protestants and Catholics, the conflict can seem as if its roots lay in differing religious beliefs. As we have seen in the first chapter, the conflict resided much more squarely in economic and political beliefs, rather than spiritual, beliefs, and the debate focused more on the best future for Ireland, rather than the best way to worship God.

Those who supported continued ties with Britain, the "loyalists," were not surprisingly those who had benefited most from those ties. They were middle- and upper-class businessmen and landowners, who controlled the majority of Northern Ireland's resources, its farmland, its factories, its businesses. They were also, for the most part, Protestants. Their philosophy had been based on hard work, determination, and taking advantage of networking and opportunities. They had immigrated to northern Ireland, principally from Scotland, in the 16th century, and were in some instances still regarded as settlers, rather than natives, by the Catholic-Gaelic population who had lived in Ireland long before their arrival.

For these other citizens of Northern Ireland, the Catholic-Gaelic population, fate had not been so kind, particularly as the 20th century began to unfold. They had suffered from economic downturns, the industries that employed them were cutting back on their labor needs, and the land they farmed was poorer quality, and required more labor-intensive care than did their Protestant neighbors'. They were largely Catholic. Their experience under British rule had left them jobless and struggling to make ends meet. It is not surprising that, as fiercely as Protestant citizens fought to maintain the status quo that gave them a comfortable living, the Catholic citizens passionately fought to change the system that, they believed, kept them oppressed.

In the treaty Michael Collins and his colleagues had helped create, Britain's plans and intent were clear. Britain wanted to retain Northern Ireland as a strategic element of the British Empire, but it was clearly preferable to have a government in place willingly allied with British interests but capable of governing itself. The plan was to create, in Northern Ireland, a government that would assume full responsibility for its citizens but consistently make decisions that would best serve British interests—where Britain would not be responsible for policing its streets or supporting its citizens but would enjoy the strategic importance of its alliance.

At the time that Ireland was first divided, Britain retained an important financial control over the north—it controlled the budget. Decisions about how much money would be spent on social services, education, law enforcement and housing required approval from Britain.

While Britain used its power over the purse, it chose to allow other decisions to be made independently. The first was political. In 1923, the Unionists took steps to ensure that they would remain the party in power, calling the shots. They changed the election rules. Where once local elections had been decided by a proportional system of representation, ensuring that both Catholic and Protestant neighborhoods were equally represented in local governments, the lines were redrawn and laws changed to require only a simple majority. In areas where the majority was in question, Catholic homes were burned or their owners threatened.

The second controversial action came with the powers vested in the Special Constabulary, a military/police force charged with keeping the peace that would soon evolve into the Royal Ulster Constabulary (RUC). The RUC was notorious for its excessive violence against troublemakers, particularly when they happened to be Catholic. Jailing without trial was common, and the brutality of the RUC was quickly apparent. The Special Powers Act, passed in 1922, gave the RUC the right to arrest and detain suspects without trial for an indefinite period of time, as well as to use any means necessary to maintain order.

The actions of the RUC and the clearly illegal rigging of elections were an embarrassment to Britain. The need for extensive social services, threatening to create a welfare state in Northern Ireland, was an equal source of concern. But a kind of solution had been achieved in the region, and British politicians would have encountered great opposition both from British citizens and the

The Special Constabulary, a military/police force, was formed in 1922 to keep the peace during the Irish Civil War. Units like this group of B Specials (shown outside Westminster Abbey in London) were notorious for using excessive force against troublemakers, particularly if they were Catholic.

Unionists in Ireland if they attempted to make any kind of extensive changes just as a settlement had seemingly been achieved. And so the Unionists were allowed to shape their own parliament, to police their streets as they saw fit, and to take steps to ensure that they remained firmly in power.

They viewed Northern Ireland as a fully separate region, known as Ulster. They did not feel part of a larger Ireland; instead they saw their region as different culturally and economically, as well as politically, from the counties to the south. The Orange Order was created, in part, to celebrate this distinct heritage. Any Unionist hoping for a career in politics joined the Orange Order as the critical first step. The Orange Order was clearly a Protestant organization, inviting Protestant pastors to serve on boards, to speak at its meetings, and to help advise on the direction of schools. There was no separation of church and state in the government of Ulster, or if there was, it was only a separation between the state and the Catholic church. Orange Order parades became a regular rallying point, both to celebrate the stamping out of the republican movement and to ensure that the anti-Catholic sentiment remained visible to all citizens.

For the Unionists, Ulster had little in common with the Irish counties in the south. They were British, proudly subservient to the British king. The opening of the new parliament at Stormont in 1932 became a proud symbol of all that had been achieved. And, the Unionists were proud to point out, it was much bigger and grander than the parliament in Dublin.

A FADING DREAM

For the Catholics of Northern Ireland in the years after partition became a reality, their struggle had resulted only in increased hardship. They were a minority, suffering discrimination and harassment when it came to jobs, housing or political representation. After the death of

The new parliament of Northern Ireland at Stormont, opened in 1932, became a proud symbol for Unionists of their political power. Standing outside the parliament building is a statue of Edward Carson (1854-1935), a Unionist leader and founder of the paramilitary Ulster Volunteer Force, created in response to the activities of the IRA.

Michael Collins, the government south of the partition line distanced itself from their struggle, focusing instead on the demands of shaping a new country. They were on their own.

In a sense, partition fractured what had up until that

time been a community—Irish Catholics—united by their faith. After the division of Ireland, Northern Catholics found themselves isolated, unwanted inhabitants in a territory marked out for Protestants wishing to remain part of the United Kingdom. The creation of a political force from this community would take time, in part because the formation of a political party and the launching of a movement would require a kind of acknowledgment that their goals of a united Ireland had not been met, and that they could not rely on assistance from south of the partition line.

Northern Ireland was, in a sense, a territory shaped by fear from its very beginning. Protestants had feared that Britain would withdraw from Ireland altogether, leaving them a minority. Irish negotiators had feared that they would achieve no independence at all, and so had been willing to settle for a divided land. Britain feared the loss of a strategically valuable territory so close to its own shores, and so had drafted a compromise that would permit independence, but only for some of the Irish.

The fear that marked Northern Ireland from the start evolved into a divided land in which there was little room for neutrality. Your religion shaped your political position; your political views clearly marked you as Catholic or Protestant.

IRA AT THE CROSSROADS

As the 1920s came to an end, the IRA wrestled with the choice about how to proceed. Economic and social problems were crippling Northern Ireland; the RUC was regularly imprisoning young men simply upon a suspicion that they might have links to the IRA. A political solution to the problem quickly became impossible, as the rearrangement of voting districts eliminated any possibility that a legal, political solution to the crisis could be achieved.

At this important crossroads, the IRA embarked on a course of violence. The violence attracted members— young men looking for excitement and desperate to strike out at the forces that were keeping them oppressed—at the same time that it made it less likely that the IRA's goals could be achieved. Once the IRA had firmly been identified with terrorist activities, few would be willing to simply hand over power to them. The violent tactics the IRA undertook would come to mark their efforts more clearly than any goals they might be working for, and it would become increasingly unclear exactly what the bombings and the assassinations were meant to accomplish. Were they working toward an end to the partition of Ireland? Greater political representation within the existing system? An end to British involvement in Northern Ireland? A solution to social problems? All of the above?

The years immediately following Michael Collins' death and partition left the IRA leadership in prison or struggling with the aftermath of the treaty. Many of them felt betrayed by the outcome, uncertain about what to do next, and frustrated that all of their efforts had left Ireland torn in two. They were angry with their leaders, who they felt had betrayed all that they were fighting for by achieving independence only for some, but not all, of Ireland.

Their view, that their aims had not been achieved, left them unable or unwilling to recognize the government in the North, its courts, its laws and its rules. The oath they had taken when joining the IRA required them to swear to defend the Irish Republic from "all enemies, foreign and domestic" and to refuse to yield to "any pretended Government, Authority, or Power within Ireland" that was hostile to the Irish Republic for which they fought. However, without recognizing the political reality of the North, the only option of change open to them was a military one. Even if they did not recognize the government in existence, they still needed to rely on political parties to help offer a political alternative to the system in power.

By the 1930s, dissastisfaction with the absence of support from leaders in the south led to a split between the IRA and the political party with whom it had long been linked, Sinn Fein. For a time, the IRA linked its efforts with other political parties. There was confusion about whether the IRA could achieve its goals merely by action alone, or in conjunction with a political party, either one that it had created or one already in existence. One party that built a relationship with the IRA during this time was the newly formed *Fianna Fail* (Warriers of Destiny), created by many of the leading political figures during the civil war who had come to the conclusion that a political compromise could be reached, that a political party could, with enough votes, take over the parliament and shape it into a legislative body that was a more legitimate representative of all the people.

The IRA at the same time was courting foreign support. America was a particularly fertile territory for funds and other offers of assistance to the Irish Republican cause. It is helpful to remember that for the many Irish Americans living in the United States in the early part of the 1900s, their own memories of prejudice and poverty were quite similar to those of the Catholics of Northern Ireland. In major American cities, Irish immigrants were crowded into slums, and had faced discrimination in jobs and housing from the Protestant upper classes. There was much sympathy for the cause, both before and after the civil war, and IRA fundraising efforts were often spectacularly successful in the United States.

In spite of this, the IRA's efforts to advance their cause seemed at times haphazard. By 1936, the Irish government was becoming concerned at the frequency of the violence, ranging from diners at a Masonic Hall in Cork being held up in the midst of a party to the assassination of an elderly admiral who had been guilty merely of providing information to young men interested in joining the British navy.

As the RUC cracked down severely on known or suspected IRA members and sympathizers, the IRA decided upon a controversial course. Lacking significant numbers to fight the battle on Irish soil, not wanting to further alienate Irish support by risking loss of Irish lives or destruction of Irish property, they decided to take the battle to Britain in a series of bombing campaigns designed to confront British officials and citizens with the consequences of their government's policy in Ireland. The campaign began in January 1939 with what amounted to a declaration of war, demanding the withdrawal of British troops from Ireland.

The explosions struck in London and other British cities, with explosions creating havoc at gas and electricity plants, telephone booths, mail boxes, movie theaters, post offices, train stations and businesses. Retaliation was quick to follow. The IRA was declared an illegal

The IRA soon took its campaign to the streets of London, bombing numerous targets including this Midland Bank, devastated by an explosion in June 1939.

organization by the government of Northern Ireland on June 14, 1939. On that same day, an act was passed (the Offences Against the State Act) creating military tribunals, special courts made up of army officers, who would oversee the prosecution of anyone thought to be trying to overthrow the existing system of government, or trying to create or support an armed force. The Irish government in the south announced its dismay at the terrorist activities and pleaded with those responsible to stop immediately.

Britain's crackdown was at least in part due to the looming presence of war threatening from the continent. It was believed by some in Britain that the IRA was being encouraged and supported by foreign involvement, including the Nazis.

BOMBINGS IN THE NORTH

As World War II swept the continent, Ireland declared its neutrality, a position viewed bitterly by Britain. Northern Ireland, as a British territory, would suffer the consequences of the war, with fierce German bombings directed at the northern counties while those south of the partition line were largely untouched by the effects of the war.

The IRA also felt the effects of the war. As Protestant and Catholic residents of Northern Ireland huddled together in air-raid shelters during the bombing of Belfast, they came together in a way that would make it less possible for them to view each other with the same hatred after the war had ended. Britain took further steps to alleviate the suffering of the north by extending welfare benefits to the territory, making it more difficult for the IRA to stir up the same level of anti-British sentiment as had been felt before.

By the war's end, the focus in Northern Ireland had shifted. No longer was its primary goal the reunification of the country under a single government. Instead the concern of most Catholics in Northern Ireland was to eliminate discrimination, and to achieve more equal political representation.

The issues that had first brought the IRA into being under the dynamic leadership of Michael Collins had become less important. The grand, sweeping ideals of a single republic, unified and independent, had been replaced by more basic needs—fair housing and health-care; a voice in local government; jobs and education. The challenge for the IRA was to listen to this shift and respond to it. The burden for Britain was to ensure that the needs of its Irish territory were addressed, while attempting the massive task of rebuilding after the war. Both sides would find the challenge nearly impossible.

WARRIORS WITHOUT A WAR

Why would someone choose to join the IRA? With each new generation, membership in the IRA has become important for different reasons, some as simple as tradition (your father was a member) or witnessing a particularly outrageous act against a brother or friend.

For some young men, it was a kind of duty. They had seen their fathers struggle for independence in the Easter rising of 1916, they had heard the stories of those who had lost their lives fighting for their vision of a unified Ireland. And now, in the aftermath of a war in which nations banded together to protect their free-doms, they were asked to swear their loyalty to the British king and allow British troops to patrol their streets. And yet there was an understanding among many new recruits to the IRA that the tactics that their fathers had used had failed. Ireland remained divided.

The division between perceptions of Ireland for this new generation began from the moment they entered school, if not before. Catholics were educated in Catholic schools, where they learned Irish history—a history that only went up to 1916—and gained from the beginning a vague sense that something tragic had happened to their nation. For Protestant students in Northern Ireland, the educational system was even less clear, teaching them almost nothing of Irish history and focusing instead on the history of Britain. As a result, contemporary events seemed to occur out of context, random violence striking because of one's religious beliefs rather than being grounded in a pattern that had been shaped by centuries of struggle.

New members of the IRA—and of the Orange Order—joined their respective sides without, for the most part, a clear sense of the roots of their conflict. The violence that crippled each side, that had claimed family members and friends, seemed even more unjust. It was as if both sides were locked in a battle without a clear understanding of the larger war that had brought them to opposing sides.

As the 1950s began, the aims of the IRA had been clarified to a simple goal: to drive British forces out of Ireland. A series of battles were launched along the border, principally by IRA forces in the south. During the war, the border had become a fertile ground for smuggling, as the North suffered from wartime rations. Everything from butter to nylon stockings became valuable goods, and the farms on either side became the site of nighttime raids, midnight border crossings by smugglers and crackdowns by customs agents.

After the war ended, the same winding roads and tiny farms became the site of raids by the IRA. From 1956 to 1962, British targets on either side of the border were attacked, but the aim of the Border Campaign, to spread the revolts from the border to the major cities north, largely failed. There were significant deaths on both sides, and the Irish government reacted with outrage against the terrorist tactics of the IRA. More importantly, public support for the aims and actions of the IRA steadily disappeared. By 1962, the IRA was forced to admit that, lacking the public support for their efforts to achieve a unified and free Ireland, there was little point in continuing the campaign. The war had finally, it seemed come to an end, and the IRA with it.

As the 1960s wound down, the IRA was split as neatly as the island of Ireland. A vote was put forward to IRA members: should they recognize the governments of Dublin, Stormont and Westminster? Recognition of the rights of these three parliamentary bodies—Dublin governing the Republic of Ireland in the south, Stormont making policy for Northern Ireland, and Westminster overseeing the actions of Stormont for the British government—would mean, in a sense, admitting that the partition of Ireland was a fact that must be accepted. It would mean the IRA and its political wing, Sinn Fein, would need to work within the system, rather than focusing on uniting all of Ireland under a single system of government. It would also provide Sinn Fein with an opportunity to participate in a larger scale within the existing political system, to attempt to spark change through political, rather than military, actions.

The choice split Republicans who had previously come together to work for a single aim. No single majority was

Sinn Fein has long been linked to the IRA as its political wing. In this photo, taken on August 14, 1955, Danny Ryan (chief recruiter for the IRA and one of its senior officers in England) speaks before a crowd at a Sinn Fein meeting held in the Camden Town section of London.

able to guarantee the decision on either side. As a result, a new "provisional" Army Council was set up, and many IRA and Sinn Fein members rallied around this new organization—a new organization sticking with the old methods of achieving their aims, through violent armed action. The IRA founded by Michael Collins would gradually slip away.

The new "Provisional IRA" (known as *Provos* by some in Northern Ireland) became the force that would push the debate about the future of Northern Ireland into the headlines. While some argued that success would only be achieved by working with the system, the Provisional IRA disagreed. They refused to recognize a system that, they felt, was unjustly thrust upon them. They would continue to fight the war—for as long as it took.

3

A Return to Arms

How did the IRA resurrect itself to become a significant, powerful presence in the politics of Northern Ireland?

With the end of the border campaign and the winding down of IRA activities, those who had fought fiercely for unity now found themselves facing more everyday issues: jobs, housing, employment. The need for a united Ireland, the glory of an independent republic, were replaced by concerns about issues that had a more direct impact on those living in Northern Ireland—equal rights.

The civil rights movement was certainly not unique to Northern Ireland in the 1960s. The call for equality was first heard in the United States, where African Americans launched a protest movement to call for a change in policy to ensure fair treatment of all in matters of education, housing, employment and other government policies. The movement spread rapidly to young people in Europe, who joined the cause for equal rights.

In Northern Ireland, the discrimination against Catholics became a rallying cry for the student movement. What had

At the age of 21, Bernadette Devlin was elected to the British House of Commons—the youngest woman ever to serve in that legislative body.

begun with marches and peaceful demonstrations soon evolved into violence, as RUC and Loyalist troops were called out to keep the peace and instead attacked the protestors. The greatest violence seemed to occur in lower-income areas, where both sides had the most to fear from the other and the most to gain from violence. For the lower-income Catholics, discrimination was a constant presence in their lives. For the lower-income Protestants, the demands of Catholic protestors—for better jobs and increased opportunities—were a threatening reminder that their own position was unstable. They feared that more opportunities for Catholics would come at their own expense. The lower-income Protestants had little, but feared losing the little they had, while the Catholics had even less.

The confusion presented an opportunity for anti-Catholic forces, many of them rallying under the banner of Reverend Ian Paisley. Paisley had established, in 1951, his own church, the Free Presbyterian Church of Ulster, which by the late 1960s had attracted nearly 15,000 supporters who followed a charismatic leader intent on preaching a message of hatred and intolerance. Paisley's focus was on the threat posed by Catholicism, both to the security of Protestants and to the security of Northern Ireland. His supporters, lashing out in violence, would claim their close ties to Britain while, in nearly every case, acting without regard for the policies or wishes of the government to which they claimed such strong allegiance.

The late 1960s brought several figures to the light— figures who spoke for those who felt underprivileged, under-represented, or threatened by forces representing a point of view different from their own. As Ian Paisley spoke out for a militantly anti-Catholic crowd, forming his own political party and seeking to ensure that those with his view were elected, other political forces arose to present a different face of Northern Ireland. One of these was a 21-year-old student from Queen's University named Bernadette Devlin.

In December of 1968, the Unionist M.P. (Member of Parliament) from the region known as Mid-Ulster—the representative the region sent to the British House of

Commons—died suddenly. A few months later, an election was called to select his replacement. The Unionists nominated his widow, a candidate who seemed all but certain to fill the seat of her late husband.

And then, Bernadette Devlin put her name forward to run for the spot. In two weeks, she and a team of young advisers put together a campaign that rallied the Catholic population and spoke to those involved in the civil rights movement. She won on a platform of social reform, and was quickly the focus of intense media attention as she took her spot in the British House of Commons, the youngest woman ever to serve in that legislative body.

Only days after her election, she made her first appearance at the House of Commons, an appearance that would make her an instant celebrity. Standing bravely amidst a crowd of older and more experienced politicians in Westminster, she spoke out against the policies that were crippling her countrymen: "I can no longer say to people who put their trust in men: 'Do not worry about it—Westminster is looking after you.' Westminster is itself at fault because it has condoned the existence of . . . and has, sitting on its benches, members of that party who by deliberate policy keep down the ordinary people."

Bernadette's story provides some interesting insight into what it was like growing up in Northern Ireland as an awareness of the need for greater equality was developing into a civil rights movement. Bernadette was born in the small town of Cookstown, near Belfast, on April 23, 1947. Her family was Catholic, but Bernadette looked back more fondly on her Protestant neighbors than on her Catholic relatives as her family experienced hardship during her youth. Hostilities between the groups were only felt when each side observed their annual marches and parades, shouting and loudly proclaiming their superiority on one day a

Only days after her election, Bernadette Devlin made her first appearance at the House of Commons, speaking out against the policies that were crippling her countrymen and, in the process, becoming an instant celebrity.

year and then packing away their stereotypes and harsh language and living in relative harmony until the next year's marches rolled around.

Bernadette was never strongly aware of her father's politics; but while he may have been a member of Sinn Fein's Republican party, he was never actively involved in the more militant actions of the IRA. Nonetheless, one day when he reached work he was informed by his employer that his working papers had been labeled "political suspect," a label that meant he could no longer be employed in Ireland. He never could determine why or by whom those words had been stamped on his working papers, but the result was that he had to travel to England for work and return home on the rare occasions when he could afford to. Like many of his countrymen, greater employment opportunities lay in England, the country many of them were struggling to separate from, rather than in their own homeland, where religious biases marked nearly every Catholic as suspect.

Bernadette's father died of a heart attack on an English train traveling to his work. She was nine years old. It was August 1956, and the IRA was just beginning a new campaign that would be marked by periodic flare-ups of violence and terrorism. Bernadette's memory of this time, shortly after her father's death, was of the sound of sirens suddenly wailing in the middle of the night, indicating that somewhere trouble was starting. Doors in the neighborhood would open, and the residents would pull on their coats, grab their guns and step out into the night. The sirens meant that either the IRA had launched an attack, or that a search was underway to hunt down suspected members of the IRA. In Bernadette's memory, the sirens would mean that the fathers of her friends were disappearing into the night, while other Protestant fathers—members of the civilian force known as the Specials created to fight the IRA—were setting out with guns to find them. It was a clear example of how the conflict sparked by the IRA was busily dividing working class neighbors into two armed communities.

Bernadette's mother died while Bernadette was a young university student. After her mother's death, Bernadette helped care for her brothers and sisters while gradually becoming active in political activities on the Queen's University campus in Belfast. At the beginning, she sympathized with the Republican cause but after some study, she recognized that the problem in Northern Ireland was not partition but rather the inequality of the current system of government. This evolution in thinking—from fighting for unity to fighting for greater equality—was one that many in Northern Ireland, including many involved in the IRA, were undergoing in the 1960s. Partition had become a reality. Social justice was becoming more important to many of the political leaders than the idea of a military overthrow of the government in place. If Northern Ireland's citizens were British by law, this new group of leaders believed, than they should be British in their standard of living as well.

Just as Bernadette was becoming interested in the civil rights movement, a civil rights march was organized and she decided to participate. The march, in the spirit of Wolfe Tone, was designed to be nonpolitical, and it started off as a cheerful parade, with the marchers singing, eating oranges, and stopping off at various pubs along the route. It was only at the end of the three-mile march, in the town of Dungannon, that the festive mood changed. The road was blocked, and police prevented the marchers from proceeding on the planned route, directing them instead toward the Catholic section of Dungannon.

For the marchers, many of whom had joined simply out of curiosity or to enjoy the fun and be with their friends, it was a sudden moment of clarity that showed that Northern Ireland had its own partition problem—the line dividing Catholics and Protestants. For those who hadn't thought about this, it was a dramatic awakening. Their peaceful, happy march was not welcome on a road that passed through Protestant businesses.

The mood turned ugly and the march organizers soon were forced to caution the crowd that women and children were in their midst. "This is a nonpolitical, peaceful demonstration," one said. "Anyone who wants to fight should get out and join the IRA." The crowd yelled back, "Where do we join?"

The organizers, realizing that they had ill-planned for any unexpected occurrences, soon left and Bernadette and many of the marchers sat in a large circle outside the city limits of Dungannon, singing protest songs for several hours until finally dispersing and walking home.

For Bernadette, the protest march provided a dramatic realization that the problems that mattered to her and the people she knew could not be solved as long as their communities were divided by religion. The political leaders she had seen, even those who had organized the march, labeled themselves politically by the religious group they represented. Their cause was either a Catholic cause or a Protestant cause.

Bernadette believed that the trouble afflicting Northern Ireland was subtler. The kind of equality she thought was needed was equality that ensured decent housing, jobs, food and healthcare to all of Ireland's citizens, regardless of what church they attended. If the people of Northern Ireland were truly British citizens, then people living in Belfast or Derry should enjoy the same benefits as those living in London or Manchester.

There would be more marches that Bernadette would join, and as the civil rights demonstrations became more frequent, the response to them because more violent. Bernadette and other students at the university decided to form their own political movement, as the existing ones were ill suited to the campaign of social justice they had in mind. The group was called People's Democracy, and its aims were clear: fair electoral boundaries, freedom of speech and assembly, a fair distribution of jobs and houses, and the end of the Special Powers Act (giving the police nearly unlimited rights to arrest and jail suspects).

Bernadette and her friends would participate in political rallies, and on many occasions she would speak passionately

To protest the cruel treatment of political prisoners in Northern Ireland, Bernadette Devlin and three members of the parliament at Stormont (John Hume, Austin Currie and Paddy O'Hanlon) launched a two-day hunger strike outside the residence of the British prime minister at 10 Downing Street in October 1971.

about the need for social reforms. She was approached to become a candidate for Parliament in part because her focus was not on exclusively Catholic or Republican issues; many believed that she could attract both Catholic and Protestant voters, be a unifying candidate, because the issues she spoke about affected both groups.

At first, she declined the offer. She had no interest in becoming a politician, and her concern was for the issues that mattered to the civil rights movement, not for the issues that would get her elected. She also feared that losing the election might weaken her cause. By the time she finally agreed to run, the election was only 15 days away, and she had not yet filed the necessary papers. Friends quickly rallied around, and a whirlwind campaign was organized, where Bernadette and her campaign team would travel to five or six meetings a day, popping in and out of various places and basically racing around the entire constituency from one small village to another, many of them so remote that they hadn't even realized an election was about to be held.

By a majority of more than 4,000 votes, Bernadette became the youngest woman ever to serve in the British House of Commons. She wasted no time in creating controversy. On her first day, the Member of Parliament from Derry, a Unionist politician, launched into a speech on the recent violent responses in his territory to a civil rights march, criticizing the civil rights leaders for their inability to prevent their supporters from breaking down into unorganized squads of hoodlums. Bernadette's first speech, made without notes, was a simple, direct response to her colleague. The problem was not Northern Ireland, she noted, the problem was Westminster.

Her clear, unadorned style of speaking made her an instant celebrity in Britain. But she never truly felt at ease in the elegant setting. To her, it was never easy to tell the Left from the Right, unless they were delivering one of their carefully rehearsed speeches. To her Parliament was little more than a stuffy club, a club whose members had forgotten what life was like in the world outside.

The celebrity Bernadette received made it more difficult for her to achieve what she had set out to accomplish. For many to whom she became a symbol of hope and change, she would become a disappointment when they realized that she could obtain another mailbox for a small village but not change Northern Ireland in a day. They were disappointed when she did not speak out more for Catholic concerns. They were upset that, in order to serve in Parliament, she was willing to swear the oath of allegiance to the British queen.

But the pivotal moment came on August 12, 1969, when the Battle of the Bogside began. It began with the traditional Apprentice Boys' Parade in Derry—a procession that celebrates the anniversary of the defense of Derry by a group of apprentices in 1689. The climate in Derry had been sectarian and violent, and many Catholic and Protestant leaders asked the government to put a ban on any march until the situation could cool down. But the government refused, and 20,000 marchers assembled in Derry. Marchers paraded near the Catholic area, calling out slurs and throwing bottles. Catholics soon responded and the fighting prompted the police to charge in with sticks, beating fighters into submission. For 50 hours, protestors constructed barricades out of pipes, stones and rubble and then fought fiercely in their own defense, hurling stones and "petrol bombs"—rags soaked in gasoline and set on fire. Tear gas filled the air.

But what was unbelievable to many in Britain was the sight of Bernadette Devlin, Member of Parliament, in the thick of the crowd, wearing jeans and a sweater and organizing squads making up the petrol bombs, then shouting at them to throw them straight at the police. As the battle waged on, civil rights marchers organized protests in ten other towns. The government responded by calling out the Specials and these civilians set to work burning down Catholic homes, and launching machine gun attacks at Catholic citizens. The British prime minister was forced to call in the British army to prevent the outright slaughter

In August 1969, the Battle of the Bogside began in Derry. Protestors constructed barricades out of pipes, stones and rubble, and the IRA set up checkpoints like this one at the entrance to the Bogside to protect Catholic homes and businesses from Unionist forces. The British army was ultimately called in to bring an end to the violence.

of Catholics. Finally, the police were forced to withdraw.

It was a moment that would change much of the political climate in Northern Ireland. Where once hatred had been kept packed away, to be brought out only once a year and paraded through the streets, it had flared out of control.

Neighbor had fought neighbor. Irish families had fought each other with violence, and only the arrival of the British army had brought the crisis to an end.

A LAND UNDER SIEGE

As Northern Ireland was crippled by the combinations of protests and violent responses, the government was faced with a crisis. It responded with strong measures, but its response seemed heavily leveled at Catholic communities. Curfews were imposed in Catholic neighborhoods, homes of Catholics were subject to random searches for suspected weapons, and more significantly, a policy of internment was imposed where people suspected of being involved in the violence (principally suspected of an involvement in the IRA) could be thrown into jail for an indefinite period of time, without a fair trial.

The policy of internment was a disaster. It clearly was one-sided. Those jailed were almost all suspected of violent IRA activities, rather than the violent Loyalist groups attacking civil rights marchers. More importantly, the British forces lacked adequate intelligence about the IRA, so that many of those jailed were innocent of any involvement in the organization while IRA leaders and active members remained at large. For those unjustly jailed and their families, the British policy demonstrated more clearly than any IRA activity that the interests of Catholics would never be protected under the existing system of government.

SUNDAY, BLOODY SUNDAY

On January 30, 1972, a crowd of 10,000 people gathered in the town of Derry to protest the British policy of internment. Although protest marches had been banned in the

On January 30, 1972, a crowd of 10,000 people gathered in Derry to protest the British policy of internment. British paratroopers on the scene fired on the crowd, killing 13 and injuring 13 others. Here, one victim of the Bloody Sunday violence is carried away by Irish civilians.

region as an effort to stem the violence, those gathered in Derry were unarmed. As the march drew to an end, the crowd began to disperse, and members of the British army began to arrest the marchers. A shot rang out—whether it was a soldier or a protestor is the subject of ongoing dispute. British paratroopers on the scene fired on the crowd, killing 13 and injuring 13 others, many of them shot in the back as they attempted to flee the scene.

The killings triggered massive outrage in Northern Ireland. The next day, 30,000 people marched to the British Embassy in Dublin, burning it to the ground to protest the actions of British soldiers.

For British citizens, the images from Derry evoked absolute disbelief and horror. In their eyes, the people of

Derry were British citizens, and so they watched in shock as British military fired upon their own people.

The chaos from the events spread as far as the British House of Commons. Outraged at what seemed to her to be a misrepresentation of the facts, Bernadette Devlin stood up in that parliamentary body and berated the British Home Secretary, Reginald Maudling, exclaiming, "The minister got up and lied to the house. Nobody shot at the paratroops, but someone will shortly . . . ." Bernadette then ran across the floor of the House of Commons and physically attacked Maudling.

The repercussions from Bloody Sunday would be felt for years. The British government felt strongly that the government in Ireland was completely incapable of maintaining control of its own people. It decided to take matters into its own hand. In March of 1972 the government of Northern Ireland was dissolved. The Stormont parliament was suspended for one year. The British government would now directly rule the territory.

For the Unionists, the suspension of their parliament—the place from which they and their supporters had governed Northern Ireland for nearly 50 years—created outrage. There was tremendous concern about exactly what the future would hold. Political chaos resulted, as some Unionist politicians threatened to set up their own provisional government, claiming that they had sworn to obey the will of the British queen, not the British parliament. Others, worried that Northern Ireland would soon be forced out of the United Kingdom and be incorporated into the Republic of the Ireland of the south, vowed to fight to ensure that Northern Ireland remained independent, even if it must become independent of Britain as well.

While the Unionists wrestled with the crisis created by the suspension of the Stormont parliament, the IRA was celebrating the events of 1972 as a kind of "year of victory." IRA members had, in early March, drawn up a series of three demands—their effort at negotiation with the British government. These demands were: the closing down of the Stormont parliament; the withdrawal of British troops from the streets of Northern Ireland to their military barracks as a first step towards complete evacuation and the agreement that the Irish people had the right to decide their own future without British involvement; and complete amnesty (freedom) for all political prisoners.

The first demand was achieved and so, in June 1972 the IRA announced that it would suspend its military activities, provided that British forces promised to do the same. These tentative steps toward negotiation were responded to by the British government, which agreed to a portion of the final demand—not complete freedom for all Republican prisoners, but they would be given a kind of special status, in which they could wear their regular clothes rather than prison uniforms and have additional visits from friends and family. By this action, which the British regarded as relatively straightforward and insignificant, the IRA would later be able to claim that Republican prisoners were not ordinary criminals but instead prisoners of war. It was an important distinction between the British point of view (that it was policing its streets and imprisoning its citizens when they broke the law) and the IRA's stand (that its prisoners were participants in an ongoing war between British military and their own soldiers fighting for their independence).

On July 7, 1972, William Whitelaw, the first British Secretary of State for Northern Ireland, and a group of British ministers held a meeting with members of the Provisional IRA in London. Among the IRA delegation was a young man who had been released from jail to attend the meeting. His name was Gerry Adams.

4

Streets Full of Sorrow

The path that brought Gerry Adams to that London negotiating table was not a straight one. Born on October 6,
1948, in Belfast, Gerry joined a family that had a tradition of
participation in the Republican cause. One year before Gerry's
birth, his father was released from prison after serving five
years for his political activities—he had been arrested at 16.
His grandfather had been active in the forerunners of the IRA,
the Irish Republican Brotherhood, and his uncles were active
in the Republican movement.

Gerry's story illustrates the difficult conditions working-
class families suffered under in Northern Ireland. When he
was born, his family of six was crowded into a tiny two-bed-
room house in West Belfast, and another sister would soon
join the family in those cramped conditions, before Gerry, his
parents and his baby sister moved to their next home. This
was a single, large room on the ground floor of a gloomy,
decaying house. On the second floor was a tap for water and
a toilet, which was shared with several families. The family

Gerry Adams would become one of the most public faces of the Irish Republican movement.

lived here for four and one-half years as two more children were born.

The conditions were difficult, but no worse than that of many poor families in Belfast, where overcrowding was a particular problem in the Catholic neighborhoods. Gerry's father worked hard, but as a former political prisoner many doors were closed to him and employment in the building industry (his field) was scarce. One of Gerry's earliest memories is of the joyous anticipation when a new housing development was built for Catholic families. Poorly constructed, lacking adequate facilities, it nonetheless seemed like paradise for the families fortunate to get one of the coveted spots in the new development. It was a joyous day for the family when they moved to this new place, and it would remain the family's home for nearly 20 years, until the British army evicted the family in 1971 as part of the new internment policies.

Gerry was educated at Catholic schools where he and his peers were required to speak Irish, even when they were outside the school. They struggled with the unfamiliar phrases and stuck to English whenever they could. If a teacher should come upon them, they would speak to each other in the words from Irish prayers or songs—the Irish words with which they were most familiar.

Despite this education in a language that was no longer commonly spoken in Belfast, Gerry remained somewhat ignorant of the division that was an unspoken part of daily life while a boy. People from the Catholic neighborhoods shopped in the Protestant stores, where having money to buy goods mattered more than where you worshipped. Nonetheless, he absorbed the understanding that, in Protestant neighborhoods, it was best not to announce your religion. If stopped by someone in authority in those communities, he would give his name as "John" rather than "Gerry"—a name that would have marked him as Catholic.

Despite these minor stirrings, it was not until he was 16 years old that a true kind of political consciousness began to become an important part of his life. It was while he was walking to school one September day that he saw something in the window of a shop opposite his school that made him rush to class, where he was greeted by excited classmates who had also seen the same amazing sight. In the shop window was the Irish flag—a flag that was illegal to display.

That evening, the Reverend Ian Paisley held a Unionist meeting where it was announced that unless the offensive flag was removed in the next two days, it would be removed by force. It was Gerry's first real awareness of the anti-Catholic movement that had been steadily building in Belfast in the 1950s, ever since Paisely founded his Free Presbyterian Church there in 1951. Paisley's efforts had spread to politics, where his Ulster Protestant Association was becoming active in nominating candidates and pursuing stridently Unionist policies.

This one small flag created a crisis in Belfast, a sign of the storm that was brewing in Northern Ireland. The RUC arrived with a force of 50 men to break down the door of the Sinn Fein office and seize the flag. In response, several thousand gathered to protest this display of political suppression, and within a few hours buses were burning, an expression of the crowd's smoldering anger. Riots soon followed, Sinn Fein put the flag back up and the RUC once more took their axes, broke into the office and seized the flag. Rioters flung petrol bombs at the RUC, the RUC responded with armored cars and water cannons. By the time the protest ended, 50 civilians and 21 RUC were injured.

While Gerry had not participated, the event had tremendous impact on him and his peers. One flag—the Irish flag—had caused this violence. Why was its display so important? Why did it compel such a dramatic response? These questions marked the beginning of a curiosity that led him to a political club where, with the

The illegal display of the Irish flag in a shop window in Belfast caused a violent protest from Protestant forces and prompted Gerry Adams to join Sinn Fein.

encouragement of his father, he folded campaign leaflets for the Republican candidate. His candidate lost but, for Gerry, it was the beginning of an awareness of and interest in politics that would carry him forward into a controversial career. Only a few weeks after the riots, the 16-year-old Gerry Adams would join Sinn Fein.

All sorts of questions began to arise in his mind. Why did they learn only English history, and not Irish history, in school? Why weren't they taught about events that had happened in their own part of the world, in Belfast? Why was one political group—the Unionists—allowed to control Northern Ireland? Why did the British support what, in Gerry's eyes, amounted to a police state, as awful in its discrimination as that of South Africa?

Gerry quickly became convinced that his school would never provide the answers to his questions. To his parents' disappointment, Gerry left school when he was 17 and went to work at a pub (a bar). The pub provided him with some income to assist his parents, and the hours allowed him to participate in Sinn Fein debates, discussions and classes—he was on his way to becoming an activist.

LOCAL POLITICS, NATIONAL CONCERNS

His earliest protests involved local issues—plans for demolishing an old neighborhood and replacing it with substandard housing. Soon he was participating in parades and marches. Afraid of offending Protestant customers at the pub, his employer fired him, but he quickly found work at another pub whose largely Catholic customers would engage in lively political discussions over their pints of beer. It became another focal point for Gerry's political education.

Life for young people in the Belfast of the late 1960s differed from that of other teens in the Republic of Ireland in the south in two important ways: religious distinctions were now becoming apparent, flaring up in ugly and violent ways; and unemployment, particularly for Catholics, was skyrocketing. Prospects were bleak. It is not surprising that so many looked for an outlet for their anger and frustration, and that the outlet they chose was often participation in the more militant political groups, both Republican and Unionist.

The character of the Republican movement was changing as Gerry became active in it. Because of internment and persecution, Sinn Fein had become a quiet and secret society, revolving around a few key families like Gerry's who had been members for several generations. Debates were frequent and heated, revolving around the best course of action both for Sinn Fein and the IRA, which had shrunk in Belfast to a total of 24 men and two guns by 1961. The focus of the Republican organization had, as we have learned, moved away from an armed struggle in the 1960s and towards the idea of achieving their aims through participation in the political process. Republicans were focusing more on social issues and, because of this, found themselves linking up with socialists, communists and others whose goals centered more on civil rights than on unity.

Gerry became the press officer for one of the Republican clubs organized in the city, writing letters to the *Irish News* under various fake names and publishing several press releases publicizing the club's opinions on various political issues. The clubs were successful in part because of their emphasis on local issues and their activism on behalf of local concerns—campaigns for better housing, for example. The importance of reunification with the counties in the south no longer mattered as much to local residents dealing with crippling economic problems, but they could understand and support a group that was actively campaigning for things that mattered to citizens, things that made their daily life a bit easier.

By the end of the 1960s, the civil rights protests were growing violent, and the RUC was fighting back with equally vicious tactics. The RUC had also identified Gerry as one of the local leaders of the Republican movement, and as protests ended in police wielding sticks against the demonstrators, Gerry and his friends began to realize that the RUC would pass by other protestors to try to get at them.

For the young men and women in Northern Ireland who banded together in these protests, there was a sense of hope, of belief that things would change. As Bernadette Devlin took her seat as a Member of Parliament, there was a belief among Gerry and his friends that

Walls and barricades can barely contain the violence that has become a part of everyday life in parts of Northern Ireland. Here, children look over the fences that divide Catholic and Protestant sections of Belfast.

they were participating in a revolution, and that with enough action, the system of power could turn their away. Their parents and grandparents were more pessimistic. They had lived through all this before. The protests would do no good. The violence would only increase and spread to engulf everyone.

The crisis in Derry proved the wisdom of the elders' position. In the wake of the conflict, British troops were dispatched to the major cities of Northern Ireland, including Belfast. The few members of the IRA in the city had almost no weapons and their numbers were insignificant.

The fighting was left to ordinary citizens, and so all over West Belfast, barricades were erected. In the absence of any assistance from the IRA, Catholics banded together to protect themselves against what they felt sure would be Unionist attacks. Crates of petrol bombs and stones from broken pavements were stockpiled, spikes were hammered into the roads, trenches were dug.

As Catholic communities prepared to arm themselves and fight to protect their neighbors and their homes, the British government dissolved Stormont. Membership in Sinn Fein and the IRA increased, while Unionist forces rallied together, as both sides wrestled with fear and uncertainty about what the future would hold. Yet there was widespread dissatisfaction with the IRA's inability to protect citizens when it mattered, at the fact that the defense of Catholic communities had been left to the citizens themselves. The civil rights movement had sprung up in response to a need from ordinary people—a need that was not being met by Sinn Fein or any of the political parties. Worse, Sinn Fein had failed to recognize, understand and respond to the changing climate the civil rights marches created.

As more than 7,000 British troops occupied Northern Ireland, there was a growing sense of dissatisfaction with the political forces that had brought them to this stage. For Gerry and other young people, the sight of armed British soldiers moving through their streets, setting up bases in their schools and other buildings, was devastating.

To many, the IRA and Sinn Fein were focusing on the wrong priorities. In December of 1969 a formal split occurred within the IRA, and Gerry was among those who walked out on Sinn Fein following the split, when it became clear that the Republican forces were divided on how to advance their cause. The Provisional IRA was set up, and many who had once fought together now found themselves divided on which army to support—the Provisional IRA or the Official IRA.

For Gerry, the split extended into his family, where his own sister sided with the Official IRA. Her fiancé was an activist in the group.

THE MILITARY PRESENCE

Life in Belfast soon took on a strained kind of normalcy, with young people still going on dates to the movies or dancing, but then hurrying to return to their own neighborhoods as soon as it grew dark. The British soldiers became a regular presence on the streets, but not one that was overlooked. Ordinary citizens listened to the army messages and the communications sent by the RUC, which could be heard on radios or, more clearly, on the police scanners that many citizens purchased.

The early army efforts were clumsily heavy handed, and even the slightest hint of protest resulted in huge amounts of tear gas being poured into an area. These actions united ordinary citizens who might otherwise not have been compelled to join the cause, directed as they were against whole communities, rather than specific troublemakers. Many of those targeted had served in the British army themselves, and so could inform and ultimately train their neighbors in the tactics the army used and the most effective way to respond.

Unfamiliar with the winding Belfast streets and many cul-de-sacs and dead ends, British soldiers often set off in pursuit of one or two protestors only to find themselves trapped on a dead-end street. They would turn back only to discover that their way out had been cut off by hastily placed barbed-wire fencing, and suddenly stones and bottles would fall down on them from the rooftops, or a group of citizens, armed with sticks or bats, would appear in the doorways and attack. These young British soldiers, sent out on what seemed like a police action to restore the peace in a British territory, found themselves viewed as an invading army facing an increasingly well-organized population who deeply resented their presence.

Membership in the Provisional IRA increased steadily as more and more young people were drawn to the military solution as the only way to ensure an end to the British army patrolling their streets. By November of 1970, the position of the Provisional army had become so powerful that it was announced that the Provisional executive and council had been replaced by a regular group of IRA officials. This formally ended the "provisional" phase of the IRA. And the battle was changing. What had been a fight between the Stormont government and Republicans fighting for their civil rights had changed. It had become a fight between Republicans and the British government.

Just as the IRA had decided that a military solution was the only possible one to effect true change, so too did the British government eventually conclude that the violence could only be brought under control with a strong military presence and tactics. In August of 1971, the number of British troops in Northern Ireland was increased to nearly 12,000. A few days later, internment was introduced.

Early in the morning of August 9, Gerry woke from a brief sleep to hear people running around and shouting. Because he was a marked man, Gerry no longer stayed at his parents' home but instead had been moving from one safe house to another. Racing outside, he went to the top of the hill, where he could clearly see the British army. He could see his parents' home, from where his father and brother were being taken to prison. The streets were full of people, of chaos and shouting, as some were being seized and others were fighting back.

Later, Gerry would learn that fighting and shooting was going on outside his parents' home. Following the arrest of his father, his mother had gathered up her younger children and a few belongings and fled the house as heavy gunfire sounded around them. It was the last time they would be in their home. British forces had rammed the house with an armored vehicle, smashed the furniture and destroyed all the belongings they had left behind.

The ferocity of the introduction of internment had been meant to put an end to the IRA. The plan was to seize all known or suspected IRA organizers and leaders and put them in prison, and in this way cripple the organization. But instead the IRA, tipped off as the raids began, went into hiding and emerged to gather together the many outraged citizens who had witnessed the seizure of friends and relatives, many of them completely innocent. Membership rose dramatically as the IRA demonstrated its willingness to defend the citizens, as it became clear that the British army had introduced a military occupation in the streets of Northern Ireland.

For Gerry, the next few months would be spent in hiding or on the run from one safe place to the next. He married, but had only a brief two-day honeymoon before separating so that he could once more slip into hiding to continue his organization efforts.

AFTER BLOODY SUNDAY

In the aftermath of Bloody Sunday, the IRA experienced an influx of money, weapons and new recruits. Much of the IRA activities were centered around Belfast, where ferocious attacks were launched against the British army and the RUC barracks. The number of dead and injured on both sides grew steadily.

In March of 1972 Gerry was arrested for his suspected involvement in Republican activities and imprisoned. He was beaten during his interrogation—his arrest had taken place during a period when the internment process was notorious for particularly brutal treatment. He was imprisoned for several months, until being nominated to serve on the committee scheduled to meet with British officials to negotiate the future of the IRA and Britain's respective roles in Northern Ireland.

Gerry was chosen because of his role as a leading Sinn Fein activist but also in part because he was not a wanted man. The British did not wish to be seen negotiating with anyone who was currently being sought by the British army—apparently negotiating with a prisoner was preferable to one who had not yet been successfully arrested.

In fact, the contrast between the two parties gathered for that meeting was striking. Representing the British interests was a Scottish landowner, a millionaire Guinness heir, and two experienced civil servants. The Republican team included a teacher, a bookies' runner, a butcher's assistant, and an occasional bar employee.

The Republican position was clear: the British government must publicly state and support the right of the people of Ireland to decide their future; British forces must be withdrawn from Irish soil by January 1, 1975; political prisoners held in Britain and Northern Ireland must be released. Both sides agreed to meet again within a week, during which time each side would respect the ceasefire but could continue to remain armed and walk the streets freely.

Sadly, it was difficult for both sides, caught in a hostile

Following the end of the 1972 cease-fire, the IRA launched a major bombing campaign in Belfast. In this photo, British soldiers survey the damage following an explosion on Castle Street in August 1977.

climate, to maintain the agreed-to cease-fire and it was only a few days after the initial meeting that fighting broke out again. It may be that the British, knowing that they could not agree to the Republican demands, did little to stamp out the RUC violence when it sprung up. It is equally possible that the IRA, sensing that the British would not agree to their demands, saw little point in maintaining a cease-fire that the other side was violating.

The violence, once the cease-fire had ended, was markedly more intense. The IRA launched a major bombing campaign in Belfast, and on the afternoon of July 21, in a period of one hour and 15 minutes, 21 IRA bombs went off in the city. Seven civilians and two British soldiers were killed, and many others were injured.

The British government responded in force. Thousands more British troops were dispatched to Northern Ireland, and soon troops with tanks, helicopters and armored cars moved into the city of Belfast. The campaign was now clearly a military operation, with the British army conducting frequent house raids and searches, and builing forts in defensive positions.

The nature of the Republican response had changed, as well. For three years, many of the citizens of Northern Ireland had engaged in a kind of popular revolution—a civil rights campaign to correct the perceived wrongs in their society. But now, with armed British soldiers occupying their cities, the tone had changed. They were now engaged in a defensive campaign, they felt—a struggle to guarantee their safety from what they viewed as an invading army.

For Gerry, this new phase would mean several months in hiding, and then, once more, prison. With so many Republicans jailed, prisons were rapidly becoming a focal point of much of the IRA and Sinn Fein organization. It would be from the prisons that the conflict in Northern Ireland would enter a new phase, a phase symbolized by political prisoners literally starving themselves to death to publicize their cause.

HUNGER AS A WEAPON

Bobby Sands was a young, athletic man who had joined the IRA at the age of 18 and was imprisoned one month later, charged with possession of a weapon found in the house where he was staying. His sentence: 14 years. He was a musician and a soccer player. He also was active in a prisoners' group that focused not merely on righting the wrongs committed against Northern Ireland's citizens outside the prison walls, but also on the inhumane treatment of those prisoners being held, often without trial, on various political charges.

One campaign, launched by a group of about 300 Republican prisoners in the spring of 1978, was a protest focused on ensuring that prisoners received "special-category status." This means that they wanted it to be recognized that they had been imprisoned because of their political activities, that what was labeled "terrorist action" was in fact their effort to defend their political position. In a sense, they wanted to be recognized as prisoners of war, rather than simply labeled as ordinary criminals.

As part of their protest, the prisoners began a unique kind of strike. They refused to wear any clothing, to wash, to leave their cells, or to use the toilet. They would cover themselves only with a blanket.

Two years later, in October of 1980, seven Republican prisoners (including six IRA members) began a hunger strike, refusing to eat until they were allowed to wear their own clothes (rather than prison uniforms) and excused from prison work. The protest ended two months later in a mistaken belief that the prisoners' requests had been granted.

In March of 1981, however, Bobby Sands claimed that efforts to increase the cooperation between prison officials and prisoners had not succeeded. He had embarked on a hunger strike a few years earlier; now, once more, he began a fast to publicize the prisoners' five demands: that they be allowed to wear their own clothing; that they be free to meet; that they be excused from prison labor; that

Bobby Sands became the most famous of a group of Republican prisoners who protested their treatment with hunger strikes. He died in prison after refusing food for 66 days. His coffin was carried to its grave by six masked members of the IRA.

they be permitted additional recreation and additional mail and visits.

Bobby Sands' hunger strike was widely publicized, and drew even greater attention when, after 40 days, he was elected to serve as a Member of Parliament. But the British government was not amused. As Sands grew weaker, British officials announced that the British government would not force medical attention on someone trying to commit suicide.

Sands felt that his hunger strike was the only way to publicize the justness of his cause—his right to be recognized as a political prisoner of an occupying army. He believed strongly that Britain was an alien force, and that armed revolution was the correct response to force out this invading army and once more return the power of deciding their own future to all Irish people.

As his hunger strike wore on, Sands wrote, "I am dying not just . . . to gain the rightful recognition of a political prisoner but primarily because what is lost in here is lost for the republic." Sixty-six days after beginning his fast, Bobby Sands died. He would be followed, over the next three months, by nine other hunger strikers who lost their lives in an effort to publicize their cause.

Speaking before the British House of Commons after the death of Bobby Sands, the British Prime Minister, Margaret Thatcher, presented the British view of the conflict. "Mr. Sands was a convicted criminal. He chose to take his own life. It was a choice that his organization did not allow to many of its victims."

5

The Political Front

The views Britain's prime minister expressed upon the death of Bobby Sands, while seemingly callous, were in fact an expression of her beliefs that the IRA was a terrorist organization whose members were intent on the violent overthrow of a system of government that had been established at the request of the majority of citizens of Northern Ireland. While admitting that violence occurred on both ends of the political spectrum, both from military Republican and Unionist groups, Margaret Thatcher's belief was that the Unionist military groups existed only in response to IRA actions, and the end of the IRA would also mean the end of these Unionist organizations.

The difference in viewpoints of the crisis begins with the very name used to identify the region. Whether you refer to the six counties as "Northern Ireland" (implying, some believe, that the six counties are an extension of the Republic of Ireland and should ultimately be reunited with them) or "Ulster" (a territory of the United Kingdom) marks you as

British Prime Minister Margaret Thatcher viewed the IRA as a terrorist organization whose members were intent on the violent overthrow of a democratically elected system of government. She would become one of the IRA's prime targets for assassination.

a supporter of either the Republican or Unionist and British point of view.

Needless to say, Margaret Thatcher referred to the territory as Ulster. Selected as prime minister in May of

1979, the conservative politician would become a figure of some controversy, known alternatively as the "Iron Lady," or in terms considerably less flattering by those who disapproved of her administration and its policies. Her attitude toward the IRA was consistent with her conservative position on economic issues and foreign affairs. In Thatcher's view, there were three goals that must be met if the IRA were to be overthrown once and for all: first, the IRA should be rejected by any and all Republicans, principally by encouraging all citizens to support the existing government in Northern Ireland; the IRA should be prevented from receiving support (arms and money) from other countries; and finally, Britain must strengthen its relations with the Republic of Ireland to ensure that borders were more carefully patrolled to prevent terrorists from slipping south and escaping prosecution.

Thatcher believed that a continued link with the United Kingdom was what the majority of citizens of Northern Ireland wished. Indeed, they had voted accordingly several decades earlier. But she recognized that the Republican position (or "nationalist" position, as she labeled it) was that majority rule would not guarantee their rights, a position the Unionist efforts at redistricting had proved valid.

Unlike some British politicians, Thatcher did not believe that the best solution was *integration*—governing Northern Ireland as a part of Britain, without any difference between the government of Northern Ireland and the rest of the UK and abandoning any attempt to restore the Stormont government. Those who supported integration believed that it would send a clear message to the IRA— Ulster (Northern Ireland) was an integral part of the United Kingdom and would be governed as such, without any room for negotiation. Thatcher disagreed, understanding that an attempt at integration would serve only to alienate nearly all citizens of the region—both the Republicans, who sought a change in their minority status, and the Unionists, who wanted to reinstate the Stormont parliament while continuing their political links with Britain.

In addition, Mrs. Thatcher was influenced by the violence the IRA had brought to British citizens throughout her time as prime minister. When she was only five months in office, the IRA had assassinated Lord Mountbatten (a close friend of the British royal family), members of his family and 18 British soldiers at Warrenpoint, all on a single day. The devastating loss had convinced her that the IRA were terrorists, but that the British approach must include not merely better security and intelligence, but also astute political moves.

These were the influences dominating the British prime minister's thinking as the crisis in Northern Ireland moved into a new phase with the launch of hunger strikes. When it was announced by several prisoners that they would begin hunger strikes unless certain conditions were met, Mrs. Thatcher's position was clear—the British government could not bow to the demands of people she viewed as terrorists, whether in response to bombs or fasts. As the deadline for the hunger strike loomed, she made one small concession—to the prisoners' request that they, as "political prisoners," be allowed to wear street clothing, she agreed not to any recognition of a special status for certain prisoners, but instead that all prisoners might be allowed to wear "civilian-style" clothing.

As the hunger strike began, the British government came under intense pressure, both domestic and international, to meet some of the prisoners' demands. But Mrs. Thatcher believed that the hunger strike represented an effort by the IRA and other prisoners to take control of

Hunger strikers like Sean O'Callaghan, a suspected IRA hit man shown in 1981, were fasting to win recognition of their "special status"—as political prisoners rather than common criminals.

the prisons, to remove authority from the prison officials and to label their crimes as "political" as a way to make them seem understandable and honorable. She felt clearly that the hunger strike represented a new campaign for the IRA—a psychological one that was as bad, if not worse, as their campaign of violence.

With the death of Bobby Sands, on May 5, Margaret Thatcher assumed a new position in the conflict. She was now one of the IRA's prime targets for assassination.

BRITAIN UNDER ATTACK

With the death of several prisoners, the hunger strike came to a tragic end. For the IRA, it was a time to take the campaign to the streets of Britain, and numerous car bombs exploded over the next several months, killing and injuring many innocent civilians. One of the worst occurred on December 17, 1983, when a car bomb exploded outside Harrods, one of the most popular department stores in London, at a time when the store was crowded with holiday shoppers. Five people, including two police officers, were killed.

In 1984, Mrs. Thatcher launched efforts to design an Anglo-Irish Agreement, a document that would clarify the position of both Britain and the Republic of Ireland to the six counties in the north. On the table were issues like the question of border security, joint authority (where both sides would assist in policing Northern Ireland), and the amending of the Constitution of the Republic of Ireland to change the idea of full Irish unity from a legal claim to an aspiration, or hope. As these plans were underway, the IRA struck again, this time targeting Mrs. Thatcher.

In early October 1984, Mrs. Thatcher was staying at the Grand Hotel in Brighton, polishing a speech that she was scheduled to deliver at a conference the next day. Just before 3:00 A.M., as she was reviewing a final official paper, a loud noise shook the room. A few seconds of silence was followed by a different sound—the sound of falling plaster. Glass from the windows had blown across the carpet, and at first Mrs. Thatcher thought it was a car bomb outside.

But she would soon learn that the bomb had exploded inside the hotel, in fact on the floors above where she was staying. An entire front section of the hotel had collapsed, and several of Mrs. Thatcher's colleagues and friends had been seriously injured or killed. The IRA claimed responsibility for the blast—a blast that they had hoped would eliminate the British prime minister. But the attempt had failed—and her position on the IRA and Irish issues would only be hardened.

RAGE AND RECRUITING

The death of Bobby Sands and the visible suffering of the prisoners who chose hunger strikes or "dirty strikes" touched a nerve in those citizens of Northern Ireland who previously might have chosen an otherwise less confrontational path. The plight of the prisoners moved many Republicans to take a more active role in the struggle.

The hunger strikers were used as a powerful recruiting tool for the IRA—a visible reminder to those who felt that Northern Ireland was at war that the struggle was not over and that those fighting it were viewed as common criminals rather than political prisoners. For those fortunate enough to live in more integrated neighborhoods, or in rural areas removed from the violence of Belfast or Derry, the hunger strikers shamed many into feeling that they should be doing more for the struggle, to honor the men who were willing to give their lives for it. For those who had once been actively involved in the Republican movement and then drifted away, either through discouragement or fear, these events energized them to once more become involved.

The hunger strikers did more than embarrass people into playing a more active role in the struggle by joining the IRA. They also influenced the Republican movement via the ballot box. Sinn Fein, the political wing of the IRA, began to

REMEMBER THE HUNGER STRIKERS

Bobby Sands   Martin Hurson
Francis Hughes   Thomas McElwee
Ray McCreesh   Keiran Doherty
Patsy O'Hara   Kevin Lynch
Joe McDonnell   Micky Devine

By the time the hunger strikes were finally called off in 1981, ten prisoners had died. This mural in a Catholic section of east Belfast commemorates those who lost their lives in Long Kesh prison.

enjoy an increasing number of electoral victories. People, certain only that they wanted to do *something* to help the hunger strikers, were casting their votes for Sinn Fein candidates in larger and larger numbers. One of these candidates was Gerry Adams, elected as the Sinn Fein representative from West Belfast to the British Parliament in 1983. That same year, Gerry would be also elected president of Sinn Fein.

It was a significant turning point in the ongoing conflict between Britain and the Republican forces of Northern Ireland. As the IRA increased in numbers, as Sinn Fein elected several candidates to political office, it was becoming clear that the Republican movement was more than a few terrorists lashing out without popular support. It was more than a military movement, offering only violence with no plans for peaceful governance of both Catholic and Protestant citizens. There was a growing number of citizens of Northern Ireland who identified with the hunger strikers, who were willing to assist the IRA, and who were electing Sinn Fein candidates to represent them.

THE ANGLO-IRISH TREATY

This change in the perception—both in Britain and internationally—of the Irish Republican movement brought increased pressure on the British government to resolve the crisis. Prime Minister Thatcher, who had initially rejected outright any role for the Republic of Ireland in assisting with the policing and government of Northern Ireland, now began to recognize that it was one of the few remaining viable options. On November 15, 1985, an agreement was signed between Garret FitzGerald, the Prime Minister (or *Taoiseach*) the Republic of Ireland, and Mrs. Thatcher at Hillsborough Castle. The signing was conducted with great ceremony and televised, intended to demonstrate the dawning of a new era in the politics of the region. Hillsborough Castle is located in a predominantly Protestant village and had, until 1973, served as the home of the governor-general, the representative of the Queen in Northern Ireland.

The agreement was intended to formalize the conclusion of months of difficult negotiations that ultimately ended with the decision that the Republic of Ireland would play a small role in governing Northern Ireland. The goal was to offer some hope to Republicans that one day the island of Ireland might be a single nation—an option that would provide a less-extreme alternative to the IRA and Sinn Fein.

But those angered the most by the Anglo-Irish Agreement

In November 1984, Margaret Thatcher met with Garret FitzGerald (center), the prime minister of the Republic of Ireland, to design an Anglo-Irish Agreement, a document that would clarify the position of both Britain and the Republic of Ireland to the six counties in the north.

were Unionists, who saw with the signing of this document that Britain might be willing to, one day, sever all ties with them. In their eyes, Mrs. Thatcher had gone from a heroine to a villain with the simple signing of her name. No longer could they claim that they were absolutely and unquestionably British citizens.

Unionist opposition further crippled Northern Ireland, through violence, protests and strikes that shut down industry. Thousands gathered to listen to people like Ian Paisley shouting out in anger at this betrayal of their interests. And then came an amazing turn of events. In December of 1985, civil servants from Dublin arrived at Stormont to begin the first meeting of the Anglo-Irish Conference. The RUC was forced to hold back violent protestors attempting to break down the gates—but these protestors were loyalists. Loyalists were soon tossing bombs at the policemen with whom they had once collaborated.

But the British government stood firm. It had not bowed to violence from the IRA. It had no intention of bowing to loyalist paramilitary groups, either.

SHOOT TO KILL

The IRA continued its campaign of violent resistance. Its targets gradually changed to focus more on the British security forces placed in Northern Ireland to police the violence from both sides. Military barracks and stations were a frequent target, and the bombing efforts changed to involve fewer but more powerful explosions.

One of the most horrific bombings occurred on November 8, 1987, when a bomb exploded at the war memorial in Enniskillen. The bombing took place on Remembrance Day, and many look upon this event as the lowest point in IRA activities. Even supporters of the IRA found themselves questioning the decision to target a gathering of innocent civilians who had gathered to mourn those who had died in Britain's wars. There was no warning—a bomb suddenly exploded at the speakers' platform in the middle of the ceremony, killing 11 people and injuring 63 others.

The backlash was immediate. The IRA was forced to publicly apologize for the action, and Gerry Adams announced at the next gathering of Sinn Fein that the accidental deaths of civilians must be stopped.

But the loss of innocent lives did not stop. In fact, the violence from both IRA and loyalist groups increased in the following months. IRA bombs extended the war zone to Gibraltar in the spring of 1988, when a changing of the guard ceremony was car-bombed. IRA bombs continued to target Britain, with explosions at train stations and the stock

By the late 1980s, the IRA was increasingly targeting the British security forces placed in Northern Ireland, particularly military barracks. In this photo, Margaret Thatcher and Commandant General of the Royal Marines Sir Martin Garrod visit Deal Barracks, following an IRA explosion that killed 10 in September 1989.

exchange. Margaret Thatcher's resignation did not stop the violence. Three months into his term as prime minister, Mrs. Thatcher's successor, John Major, was sitting in the Cabinet Room at Number 10 Downing Street when an IRA bomb exploded in the garden. On April 10, 1992, a large explosion struck London's financial center. By 1993, a Gallup Poll indicated that only 27 percent of British citizens wanted Northern Ireland to remain a part of the United Kingdom.

6

The Peace Process

The nature of the IRA campaign and the character of the volunteers who made up this army—intensely committed, driven by their own experiences with discrimination and their passion for the cause—meant that targets had to be chosen for their symbolism and for the opportunity they presented. Mistakes were frequently made, innocent people were killed, bombs exploded at the wrong time or in the wrong place. For some, Gerry Adams included, the time had come to seek a political solution, rather than a military one.

This position was supported by the steadily increasing violence on both sides. A kind of stalemate had been achieved. An IRA bomb would explode. Loyalist paramilitary groups would respond, targeting a Catholic neighborhood. British military forces would police the streets. The idea of a military solution to the crisis in Northern Ireland no longer seemed possible, at least not in the short term.

Sinn Fein's political successes led some to believe that the political solution was the only one that made sense. Beginning in

John Hume, the leader of the non-violent Social Democratic and Labor Party, became one of the leading architects of the peace movement in Northern Ireland. His efforts would win him the Nobel Peace Prize.

1988, Gerry Adams, representing Sinn Fein, and John Hume, the leader of the non-violent Social Democratic and Labor Party (SDLP), began a series of meetings to try to carve out a path toward peace. For five years, the two leaders met off and on, trying to reach some sort of consensus over such issues as the British government's willingness to recognize Irish national rights and its willingness to end partition, and the likelihood of getting a majority of people in Northern Ireland to agree to any decisions that would move in that direction.

In April of 1993, Gerry Adams and John Hume released the first of what would be several statements about their respective positions and the areas of agreement they had finally reached. Their basic areas of agreement were the right of Irish people to determine how to govern themselves; that a lasting peace depended on the consent of unionists, but that unionists could not veto British policy; and that the British government must side with those attempting to find a peaceful solution to the crisis. The responsibility was firmly placed on the governments in London and Dublin to ensure that progress was made to follow through on this peace process.

The IRA responded to the Adams-Hume agreement, indicating that peace would be possible if the political will existed. The Irish Republic's government in Dublin also indicated its support for the plan. But the British government was less supportive. The key point of disagreement was the idea of how a majority of support for the idea of a united Ireland would be counted. In the Adams-Hume proposal, a referendum would be voted on simultaneously, in both the North and South, and the majority of both areas would determine whether or not partition would end. The British government, however, felt that Northern Ireland alone should decide its fate, and that the wishes of its people would be determined by counting the votes of the citizens of Northern Ireland, regardless of how the rest of Ireland voted.

Despite these areas of disagreement, there was widespread

popular support for a political solution. On December 15, 1993, the leaders of Britain and the Republic of Ireland, John Major and Albert Reynolds, made a joint statement at Downing Street, promising to begin negotiations with Sinn Fein if the IRA would call off its military campaign. The first several months of 1994 were marked by increased violence on both sides, with loyalist forces responding to IRA attacks and vice-versa, until on August 31, 1994, the IRA, responding to intense pressure to try for peace, announced that it would begin a "complete cessation of military operations" at midnight.

Sinn Fein was not immediately admitted to the negotiating table. The British government demanded that Republican forces begin the process of turning over or destroying their weapons, arguing that if the cease-fire was indeed permanent, as promised, than there was no need for them to arm themselves.

Loyalist forces responded to the changing climate with increased violence. Protestants felt increasingly alienated from the political process that was determining their future. They sought the same path that the IRA had chosen: violence. The British government was forced to issue a public statement reassuring loyalists that no "secret deals" had been arranged and that no final solution had been reached, before the loyalist paramilitary cease-fire was declared on October 13, 1994.

The peace process was fragile, and it was not easy for those who had spent so many years fighting to simply lay down their weapons. Both unionists and nationalists were suspicious of each other's cease-fire, and equally suspicious of reassurances from the British government. To try to hold the peace process together, the British and Irish governments published, in February 1995, their joint discussions, titled *Frameworks for the Future*. The key points involved the

British government's proposal for a single house of representatives, consisting of 90 members elected by popular votes, and the plans for increased cooperation between Northern and Southern Ireland.

The Unionists rejected the proposal and made it clear that they had no intention of supporting a process that, they believed, would lead to a gradual evolution into a single "government of Ireland." They argued that Britain must make it clear if it intended to formally transfer power over Northern Ireland to the Republic of Ireland but, more importantly, they demonstrated that they would oppose such a move with any means available to them.

In September of 1995, David Trimble became the leader of the Unionist Party. Trimble's initial goal had been to set up some sort of conference or assembly where issues could be formally debated between representatives of the Unionists and Sinn Fein, as a way to begin to pursue the democratic process without violence on either side. However, Trimble soon made clear his belief that the IRA was the obstacle to these kinds of talks because of its unwillingness to turn over weapons.

THE MITCHELL REPORT

In an effort to maintain the peace process, an international group was created, chaired by the former U.S. senator George Mitchell, to pave the way toward talks between all political parties by addressing the issue of paramilitary groups and the feasibility of their turning over their weapons. The report was released in January 1996. Its conclusion was that it was not possible to expect all paramilitary groups to turn over their weapons before the date set for all-party talks (February 1996). It suggested instead a compromise between the British position (all

In September 1995, David Trimble became the leader of the Unionist Party. His key role in the Good Friday Agreement would result in him receiving the Nobel Peace Prize (with John Hume). He would eventually be elected first minister of the power-sharing government known as the Northern Ireland Assembly.

weapons must be turned over before talks could be held) and the Sinn Fein position (weapons would be turned over after the talks).

The Mitchell Report proposed that all parties involved

U.S. senator George Mitchell chaired an international group working to pave the way toward peace talks by addressing the issue of paramilitary groups and the feasibility of their turning over their weapons. The Mitchell Report, detailing their recommendations, was released in January 1996.

should consider handing over some weapons during the process of talks, and that rather than setting such specific pre-conditions, the focus instead should be on involving all parties to the talks in pledging their support for basic principles of democracy and non-violence. The goal of the talks should be for the parties to commit to begin to disarm paramilitary groups, to peacefully solve political issues, and to agree to abide by the terms reached in the all-party negotiations.

The British government and the Unionist Party both put their own spin on the report, but the IRA responded with action. On February 4, 1996, the cease-fire ended when an IRA exploded a bomb in an underground parking garage in London, killing two men and injuring more than a hundred. The IRA claimed that the British government was responsible for ending the cease-fire by making it clear that it would continue to place its own interests above those of the people of Ireland. The British government responded by indicating that it would never bow to threats. The Unionists noted that the explosion proved what they had been saying all along—the IRA was never serious about peace or the cease-fire.

THE GOOD FRIDAY AGREEMENT

The conflict between Britain and Northern Ireland has been remarkable in its ability to haunt succeeding governments. The rise of the Labor Party to power in Britain's 1997 elections brought a new prime minister, Tony Blair, to the negotiating table.

On Good Friday 1998, a new agreement was reached to develop a power-sharing system of government, one that would give a voice to the political parties within Northern Ireland, while ensuring that the British and Irish Republic governments also played a responsible role in developing a peaceful and reasonable solution to the conflict. The proposal would involve a government in which power would be shared based on party strength. Key government posts would be distributed similarly—based on party strength. Parties with links to paramilitary groups (principally Sinn Fein, the Ulster Democratic Party and the Progressive Unionist Party) would be allowed to participate in the political process, provided that they maintained cease-fires and took steps to hand over their weapons.

While Tony Blair and Bertie Ahern, the Taoiseach of the Republic of Ireland, had been deeply involved in the details of the agreement, it was more fully the work of David Trimble and John Hume, who won the Nobel Peace Prize for this achievement. A copy of the agreement was delivered to every household in Northern Ireland, and it was then put to a vote. In May of 1998 the agreement was approved both in the north and south. Even voters who defined themselves as unionist voted for it by a narrow majority.

The power-sharing arrangement is tenuous. The issue of turning over weapons has remained a difficult one, as the IRA's policy of "not an ounce, not a bullet" has conflicted with Unionists refusal to participate until at least some weapons are turned in.

But these tentative steps toward a more unified system of government offer hope to those who believe that a political solution to "the Troubles" in Northern Ireland is the only possible path toward peace.

PERSPECTIVE ON PEACE

The conflict that first divided Ireland and then split Northern Ireland into pieces continues to claim lives and create chaos. The power-sharing government first put in place in 1998 has provided a solution, but it is a shaky

John Hume (right) and David Trimble display their awards following the 1998 Nobel Peace Prize ceremony in Oslo, Norway.

one. David Trimble has twice been elected to serve as first minister of the four-party coalition, a position that requires support both from Protestant and Catholic voting groups. But an administration that has been forced to shut down several times for various crises—including the IRA's refusal to disarm—is far from stable. A breakthrough occurred in October of 2001 when the IRA agreed to begin disarming in cooperation with an independent panel set up to oversee the disarmament process, but the success of the power-sharing arrangement will heavily depend on the IRA's willingness to continue to turn over its weapons.

The power-sharing arrangement has been able to proceed because its leadership has been largely moderate. It is amazing to see a government in Northern Ireland where the first minister is a Protestant, the second most powerful political leader is a moderate Catholic, and two Cabinet positions are held by representatives of Sinn Fein.

But many of the same figures and beliefs that first pushed Northern Ireland into a period of intense violence are still waiting in the wings. Following the vote that concluded with David Trimble's re-election as first minister in 2001, rival politicians began pushing and shoving each other, physically scuffling as each side attempted to get more space in front of the television cameras in the Stormont building's foyer.

The British government maintains its position that the will of the majority of Northern Ireland must be consulted before it can consider making any kind of constitutional change in the status of the territory. However, it has proceeded with plans to cut the number of forces in the territory following the IRA's announcement in October 2001 that it would begin disarming.

These are hopeful signs. And yet the violence simmering just below the surface has not yet been stamped out by political progress. In September of 2001, religious tensions flared in an unexpected and frightening fashion. Young Catholic schoolgirls in Ardoyne were terrorized as they walked to their elementary school by their Protestant neighbors, who insulted them and then threw rocks and homemade grenades at them. The picture of young girls, crying as they ran through a line of jeering adults, was a devastating indictment of how far Northern Ireland must go if peace is to become a reality. Ultimately, armored personnel carriers, British soldiers and riot police needed to be called in to line the narrow streets, simply to allow the young girls to pass peacefully from their homes to their school.

The conflict between Britain and the IRA, between the IRA and Unionist paramilitary groups, between Unionists

Religious tensions continue, despite political progress. In 2001, young Catholic schoolgirls in Ardoyne were terrorized as they walked to their elementary school by Protestant neighbors, who insulted them and then threw rocks and homemade grenades at them. Here, British soldiers and police form a protective guard so that students and their parents can safely return home from school.

and Republicans, and between Catholics and Protestants has claimed many lives. Those who have grown up in a climate of violence and hatred have found it difficult to accept small, tentative steps as real progress. There is a sense that the conflict has seeped into the soil, infecting all aspects of life in Northern Ireland.

Many questions remain. What role should Britain play in the future of Northern Ireland? How critical is the

IRA's complete disarmament to political progress? Will the voices of moderation be more influential than those of more extremist groups? When decisions are made about the future of Northern Ireland, should only its citizens have a voice and a vote, or should the voices of those in the Republic of Ireland also play a role in the decision process? If a majority group has demonstrated prejudice and discrimination against a minority group of citizens in the past, can that majority be trusted to determine the future of all people in the territory?

As these questions demonstrate, there are no easy answers to the conflict in Northern Ireland. All sides are united in their wish for peace. But they differ greatly on the path they believe will lead there.

1916 Easter Rising begins Ireland's struggle for independence.

1919 Newly formed Irish Parliament meets; IRA is formed.

1921 Michael Collins and colleagues meet with British representatives to carve out treaty for independence.

1922 Treaty is passed. Michael Collins is assassinated by Republicans.

1932 Parliament at Stormont opens.

1939 IRA begins bombing campaign in England. IRA is declared an illegal organization by government of Northern Ireland.

1956–1962 IRA wages Border Campaign.

1969 Bernadette Devlin is elected to British Parliament. Battle of the Bogside occurs. Provisional IRA is established.

1971 Internment is introduced.

1972 Bloody Sunday claims 13 lives. Britain dissolves government of Northern Ireland.

1981 Bobby Sands begins fatal hunger strike, is elected to British Parliament.

1983 Gerry Adams is elected president of Sinn Fein.

1984 IRA explodes bomb in Grand Hotel in Brighton, targeting British prime minister.

1985 Anglo-Irish Treaty is signed.

1987 IRA bomb explodes at Enniskillen, killing 11 civilians.

1994 IRA begins cease-fire.

1996 Mitchell Report is released. IRA cease-fire ends.

1998 Good Friday Agreement is approved. Power-sharing government begins.

2001 IRA agrees to begin disarming.

PRINT SOURCES:

Adams, Gerry. *Before the Dawn*. New York: William Morrow and Co., 1996.

Collins, Eamon and McGovern, Mick. *Killing Rage*. New York: Granta Books, 1997.

Coogan, Tim Pat. *The IRA: A History*. Niwot, CO: Roberts Rinehart Publishers, 1993.

Coogan, Tim Pat. *The Man Who Made Ireland*. Niwot, CO: Roberts Rinehart Publishers, 1992.

Devlin, Bernadette. *The Price of My Soul*. New York: Alfred A. Knopf, 1969.

Hastings, Max. *Barricades in Belfast*. New York: Taplinger Publishing Co., 1970.

Hennessey, Thomas. *A History of Northern Ireland: 1920-1996*. New York: St. Martin's Press, 1997.

Keogh, Dermot. *Twentieth-Century Ireland: Nation and State*. New York: St. Martin's Press, 1994.

Mackay, James. *Michael Collins: A Life*. London: Mainstream Publishing, 1996.

Mitchell, George J. *Making Peace*. New York: Alfred A. Knopf, 1999.

Pogatchnik, Shawn. "After Belfast death, a time to pray," *The Philadelphia Inquirer*, September 8, 2001, p. 2.

Ruane, Joseph and Todd, Jennifer. *The Dynamics of Conflict in Northern Ireland*. New York: Cambridge University Press, 1996.

Taylor, Peter. *Loyalists: War and Peace in Northern Ireland*. New York: TV Books, 1999.

Thatcher, Margaret. *The Downing Street Years*. New York: HarperCollins Publishers, 1993.

Townshend, Charles. *The British Campaign in Ireland*. New York: Oxford University Press, 1975.

WEB SITES:

www.bbc.co.uk

www.irishnews.com

www.irlnet.com/aprn

www.thetimes.co.uk

www.britannica.com

www.irish-times.com

www.msnbc.com

www.worldbook.com

BOOKS:

Adams, Gerry. *Before the Dawn.* New York: William Morrow and Co., 1996.

Buscher, Sarah and Ling, Bettina. *Making Peace in Northern Ireland.* New York: The Feminist Press of the City of New York, 1999.

Collins, Eamon and McGovern, Mick. *Killing Rage.* New York: Granta Books, 1997.

Devlin, Bernadette. *The Price of My Soul.* New York: Alfred A. Knopf, 1969.

Mitchell, George J. *Making Peace.* New York: Alfred A. Knopf, 1999.

Taylor, Peter. *Loyalists: War and Peace in Northern Ireland.* New York: TV Books, 1999.

Thatcher, Margaret. *The Downing Street Years.* New York: HarperCollins Publishers, 1993.

WEB SITES:

www.bbc.co.uk

www.irish-times.com

www.thetimes.co.uk

www.irishnews.com

www.msnbc.com

www.worldbook.com

page:

6:	Courtesy the CIA	59:	Hulton Archive
8:	AP/Wide World Photos	63:	AP/Wide World Photos
10:	Hulton Archive	66:	Courtesy the CIA
12:	AP/Wide World Photos	69:	AP/Wide World Photos
15:	Hulton Archive	75:	Hulton Archive
19:	© Underwood & Underwood/Corbis	78:	AP/Wide World Photos
22:	AP/Wide World Photos	81:	AP/Wide World Photos
25:	Courtesy the CIA	84:	AP/Wide World Photos
27:	AP/Wide World Photos	87:	AP/Wide World Photos
32:	Hulton Archive	89:	Hulton Archive
34:	Hulton Archive	91:	AP/Wide World Photos
39:	Hulton Archive	93:	AP/Wide World Photos
44:	Hulton Archive	97:	AP/Wide World Photos
47:	AP/Wide World Photos	98:	AP/Wide World Photos
50:	Hulton Archive	101:	AP/Wide World Photos
54:	Hulton Archive	103:	AP/Wide World Photos
57:	Hulton Archive		

HEATHER LEHR WAGNER is a writer and editor. She has an M.A. in government from the College of William and Mary and a B.A. in political science from Duke University. She is the author of two additional books on the Middle East—*Iraq* and *Turkey* in the Creation of the Modern Middle East series. She is also the author of *The IRA and England* in the People at Odds series.